Feasting on the Word®

CHILDREN'S SERMONS
FOR YEAR C

Feasting on the Word®

CHILDREN'S SERMONS FOR YEAR C

Carol A. Wehrheim

WJK WESTMINSTER
JOHN KNOX PRESS
LOUISVILLE · KENTUCKY

First edition
Published by Westminster John Knox Press
Louisville, Kentucky

15 16 17 18 19 20 21 22 23 24—10 9 8 7 6 5 4 3 2 1

Book design by Drew Stevens
Cover design by Lisa Buckley Design

Library of Congress Cataloging-in-Publication Data

Wehrheim, Carol A.
  Feasting on the word children's sermons for year C / Carol A. Wehrheim.
    pages cm
  ISBN 978-0-664-26109-2 (alk. paper)
  1. Children's sermons. 2. Common lectionary (1992). Year C. 3. Church year sermons—Juvenile literature. 4. Preaching to children. I. Title.
  BV4315.W355 2015
  252'.53—dc23

                                                        2015003416

∞ The paper used in this publication meets the minimum requirements of the American National Standard for Information Sciences—Permanence of Paper for Printed Library Materials, ANSI Z39.48-1992.

*For all the children who have listened to my stories
and helped me polish my storytelling gifts*

Contents

LENT

EASTER

SEASON AFTER PENTECOST

Stories for Special Sundays

Acknowledgments

A number of years ago, I saw a notice of a storytelling workshop to be held on the Princeton University campus. It was a week-long seminar led by Susan Danoff. I didn't know Susan, but I wanted to know more about storytelling in the hope that I, a curriculum writer and editor, could find ways to write more engaging Bible stories for children. What I discovered in Susan was not only a spellbinding storyteller but an excellent educator. I have described that week as the best week of continuing education I have experienced. From that seminar I learned not only how to tell a story, but I also discovered the power of story. Since then, I have come to believe, with more and more certainty, that the church must regain its storytelling history, telling the story to one another, face to face.

Many of the stories here are based on stories in the *Feasting on the Word* curriculum. Although I have written or revised them all, I have often been helped by a turn of phrase or point of view that was drawn from one of the writers for this series. I am especially indebted to Sharon Harding, who wrote many of the summer sessions and who gave me lovely words to begin as I wrote the Bible stories to tell to the congregation. Without the suggestion from David Maxwell that this book would be helpful to congregations, these stories would not be written down for others to tell.

There are few things I would rather do than tell Bible stories to children in church school or vacation Bible school or to the congregation in worship. I hope you will discover what joy can be found in giving these stories to others, whatever the age, and how it enriches the depth of your Bible study and faith.

Introduction

The Importance of Stories

"Children, come join me for the story," the storyteller beckoned, with arms open. Girls and boys hurried forward to get a spot next to a friend. Some children hesitated, holding a parent's hand, as they walked slowly to the front of the sanctuary. When everyone was settled, the storyteller began, "Long, long ago, even before Jesus was born. . . ." You could feel the congregation, adults and children, relax and settle in to hear the story. A good story, told well, has something for everyone, from four to ninety-four and beyond. Certainly the Bible is filled with good stories. And worship is an occasion for all generations to hear the story together. Hearing the story together is no small thing, for we Christians are a storied people, and hearing it at the same time and in the same space brings all generations together.

Many reasons are given for including a children's sermon or time with the children in the order of worship. At one end of the spectrum, it functions as a way to transition the children from the worship service to their church school classes. In that case, the little talk or story may have nothing to do with anything else that takes place in worship or in what children do in their church school classes. Too often, it is a story or talk that is prepared hurriedly and ends with a moral, one that is often beyond the understanding of the children.

But let's back up for a moment. Why is storytelling of any kind important? Stories—family stories, community stories, national stories, faith stories—are how we pass values from one generation to the next. These stories tell us who we are and what is important to our family, our tribe, our nation, our faith community. These stories bind us together. In this same way, Bible stories bind us together as the people of God. They tell us who we are and whose we are. They help us see God at work in our world. They incorporate us into the body of Christ. And stories begin to work this wonder when we are very, very young. Therefore, what better time to tell Bible stories on a regular basis than when the faith community is gathered in its most unique and faithful act, the worship of God?

When the Bible story matches the sermon text, the story provides an entry point into the sermon for adults and children as they ponder the story and how it is proclaimed in the sermon. Repetition of the story as it is told and as it is read from the Bible reinforces the text, its structure and plot, and need not be a concern for worship planners.

When that text is also the passage studied in church school, for children or all ages, which is possible with a lectionary-based curriculum such as *Feasting on the Word,* the possibilities for faith formation are multiplied. But these optimal conditions are not necessary to nurture faith through telling Bible stories in worship.

The ultimate goal is to tell the Bible story so the listeners' imaginations and hearts catch fire, as happened to the disciples on the road to Emmaus when Jesus told the stories of the prophets. Bible stories help us recognize Jesus and meet the God who sent him to us.

Another reason for telling Bible stories in worship is to free these stories from the page. When Moses spoke to "all Israel" as the people were about to enter the Promised Land without him, he told them that everyone was responsible for teaching the children, and this was no small thing, "but rather [their] very life" (Deut. 32:47). Every adult in the church has some responsibility for telling the story to the next generation. Indeed, the congregation promises that to each infant baptized. When the story is told in worship, adults have a model to follow. They find that it's just fine to laugh at a humorous detail or to wonder what happened next. They also learn that they don't have to include every word or get everything right. After all, this is how Bible stories were passed from generation to generation, by word of mouth from one person to the next. Not every adult will tell the story to the congregation but might tell it to one or two children or grandchildren.

Everyone is a storyteller. Think about it. When you find a bargain at the mall and phone a friend to tell about it, you are telling a story. When a child asks, "What was school like when you were in second grade, Grandmom?" and you tell about your second-grade classroom, you are telling a story. Stories help us know one another—our dreams, our fears, and our joys. We may not all be comfortable telling stories before a group, of children or adults, but we are all storytellers, and some of us are called to be storytellers of the church's story to the congregation, the whole congregation.

One more thought about telling Bible stories in the service

of worship. If you have heard StoryCorps on a public broadcasting station, you know that personal stories can delight, enlighten, heal, and bridge gaps in relationships. David Isay, the originator of StoryCorps, describes the stories collected as conversations in sacred space. No, they are not recorded in a religious building, but the stories are the meeting of two souls with a facilitator, whose task is to listen, listen intently, to bear witness to the story and storyteller. Perhaps the adults in the congregation are the silent witness to the story when it is told in worship. If that is the case, adults are included in the audience for the story. It's not for children only.

For all of these reasons, about the importance of story and the place Bible stories have in nurturing the faith of all ages, perhaps we ought to think of the time when children come forward as a time to tell the Bible story in worship rather than a "children's sermon" or time with the "children." The story is for everyone present; it's just that the children get a front row seat. It's a story, not a sermon. Thinking of this worship element as a children's sermon has fostered too many pious talks that end with a moral. Or children are subjected to an object lesson before they are able to comprehend metaphor, and they become fixated on the object. Occasionally something said leading up to the story distracts children from even hearing the story. Many years ago, a person giving the children's sermon began by telling the children that he had hit a deer on the way to church. A mother reported later that her boys could talk about nothing else the rest of the day. Did they hear the message of the children's sermon? Probably not. Tell the story. Tell it with all the enthusiasm and delight that you can muster so that God's Word is given to each person in the sanctuary.

Preparing the Story

This book provides a story based on one of the lectionary texts for each Sunday, from the first Sunday of Advent to Reign of Christ/Christ the King Sunday (the end of the church year), as well as a story for Christmas. Also included are four stories for special times in the congregation's life. Each story is about five minutes long.

To prepare to tell one of the stories provided here, read the Bible text that inspires the story as well as the story itself. Adapt the story so the style and the words or phrases are comfortable for you. Don't try to memorize it word for word. You are *telling* the story, not reciting it.

Practice telling the story over and over. Tell it to a mirror, to your pet, to anyone who will listen. As you tell it again and again, you will find phrases and word combinations that are natural for you; but keep the language simple and appropriate for children. Then it is appropriate for those adults who are listening intently too. Keeping the language and concepts simple doesn't mean it will be boring for youth and adults. A story told with enthusiasm will draw in the entire congregation.

As you practice telling the story, notice how your arms or head move naturally to the emotions or content of the story. Perhaps you stand tall and strong to emphasize the power of Jesus when he calms the storm. Or you might shield your eyes and look into the distance as you tell about the lost sheep. If you find motions difficult, pantomime the story, using actions and no words. You may discover some natural movements in the process.

With a longer story, you may find it helpful to get the

scenes firmly in your mind. One method is to outline the story and remember the outline by memorizing the opening words for each scene.

Have the opening and closing sentences firmly in mind. This is an exception to telling, not memorizing, the story. Knowing how you will begin and end relieves some of the stress. Being prepared with a strong concluding sentence will keep the story from drifting away from you and the listeners.

When telling the Bible story, sound practice suggests that you do not ask a question of the children. Someone will answer you, and more often than not the answers will provoke a chuckle from the congregation. Too many children have been hurt by that ripple of laughter, because they answer with all seriousness. The better road is to avoid asking questions.

Occasionally, a child will ask a question in the middle of the story. For example, a girl of about seven asked, "What does 'getting even' mean?" The story was about the rules from God in Leviticus 19, and the storyteller said, "When someone is mean to you, don't try to get even." The storyteller, in a sentence, explained "getting even." The child responded, "Oh, I thought maybe it was getting everything right." One can understand why a child might think that. Such distractions and other kinds will happen. Take them in stride and try to keep your focus.

Telling the Story to the Whole Congregation

Everyone comes along when a story is told well. And most people, with practice, can learn to tell a story well. Here are some things to consider:

Stand facing the congregation with the children facing you. Sitting in the congregation and listening to a disembodied story, when you know the storyteller is using motions and movement, is distracting. Encourage the children to look at you by saying something like, "Sit so I can see your eyes."

Look at the children and focus on one child who is eagerly waiting to hear the story for a moment. Then begin with the opening sentence you carefully crafted.

When the story includes a quoted section from the Bible, as in a letter from the New Testament, write or type the quotation. Roll it up like a scroll and open it to read during the story. Or place your paraphrase in the Bible and open it to read the paraphrase. Use a Bible that the children will recognize so that they know that what you are reading is from this very book.

While motions and movement can contribute to the excitement and action of the story, try to keep your own actions to a well-selected minimum. Too much movement is distracting. Constant pacing back and forth makes listeners dizzy.

At the end of the story, after you have said that carefully prepared closing sentence, hold the gaze of a child who has been listening intently for just a moment before praying.

Enjoy telling the story. What a wonderful gift you are giving to each person who is listening, whether this is the first time a child has heard it or the adults know it backward and forward. But that's the wonderful thing: the story you tell may invite adults familiar with it to look at the words from another angle. The wondrous thing about the Bible is that there is always more to say and ponder.

Writing Other Bible Stories to Tell to the Congregation

Sometimes the lectionary texts aren't what you want, or the sermon text is not from the lectionary. Then the storyteller is responsible for writing a story. The story "Queen Vashti" (p. xv) was written for that reason, since Esther 1 never appears in the Revised Common Lectionary. Once the text is chosen, follow these steps.

1. Read at least one commentary on the passage. Look for interpretations or information that will guide how you approach the story. For example, if the story text is from Philippians, explain that Paul wrote this letter to the church in Philippi while he was in prison. For the story of Queen Vashti, notice how the story begins, because it is difficult to date the book of Esther and because it was certainly written long after the events it records.

2. Read the text in several translations, including one with a limited English vocabulary (CEV or Good News). Notice how the translations differ and where they are alike or similar. If you are the preacher and the storyteller, steps one and two will serve for the sermon preparation and the story preparation. The other steps may also help you move into the story as you begin your sermon preparation. Be open to the possibility.

3. Tell the story to yourself. If you aren't sure of the sequence, just keep going. This will help you establish a rhythm for the story and identify the parts of it that are important and memorable. Go back to the text and see what you missed or added.

4. Write the story as you would like to tell it. One of the most difficult things about writing the story is selecting

words that convey meaning to the children. Bible stories are not occasions to show off your vocabulary or clever phrasing, for children or adults. This is a rough draft. Pay no attention to grammatical details, misspelled words, or sentence structure.

5. Compare your written story to the text. Add missing details that are important to the story. Can you add details that will enliven the storytelling without compromising the text? Check on the sequence of events. Is your story faithful to the text and what you know about it from reading the commentary? If you compare "Queen Vashti" to Esther 1, you will soon notice details that are not part of the story, such as the names of the king's eunuchs and the details about the drinking party. Yet the essence of the story and Vashti's role in setting up the necessity for a new queen come through clearly.

Generally, you can omit details that are inappropriate for children without damaging the intent of the story. For example, in Year B, the Gospel lectionary text for Proper 20 is Mark 9:30–37. Verses 30–32 are Jesus' prediction of his death, while verses 33–37 tell of Jesus' conversation with the disciples about who is the greatest. When preparing the story for telling in worship, base the story on verses 33–37. Omitting the first three verses doesn't change the story of Jesus and the disciples reaching Capernaum. When you look at that text carefully, it is two stories. As a rule of thumb, keep to one story for this moment in worship.

6. The opening and closing sentences of the story are especially important. Write the opening sentence carefully to get the attention of the listeners right away. Look at "Queen Vashti" (below) and notice how the opening sentence tells the listeners that this is a story from the Old Testament, a

story that Jesus may have heard as a child. The words "A very long time ago, way, way longer than anyone here can remember" draws listeners in to hear how the story unfolds. The closing sentence is just as important because it may help the listeners remember the story and help you draw the story to a close. This is not a moral or explanation of the story; it is the conclusion of the story. Look at "Queen Vashti." The closing sentence encourages the listeners to ponder the story on their own and clearly marks that this is the end of Vashti's story. Indeed, nothing more is said about her in the book of Esther. If you read Esther 1, Vashti's story doesn't have an ending. The closing sentence of the story doesn't provide an ending either, but it does provide a way to end the story being told.

Now you are ready to rehearse. As suggested earlier, rehearsal of the story will make all the difference in your role as storyteller. Tell the story aloud often. Let your body move naturally to the story's emotions and content. If you find motions difficult, try pantomiming the story; or if you enjoy drawing, sketch the story in scenes. You may discover some natural movements in the process. And memorize the opening and closing sentences so you have them firmly in mind. Incorporate them into the story so they sound natural.

Writing a Bible Story for Telling

1. Read a commentary on the story text.
2. Read the text in several translations.
3. Tell the story without referring to the text.
4. Write the story as you want to tell it.
5. Compare the story to the text and revise.
6. Write the opening and closing sentences.

Queen Vashti

A very long time ago, way, way longer than anyone here can remember, King Ahasuerus ruled over all the land from Ethiopia to India. He wanted to show all the important men of those countries just how rich and important he was, so he had a big feast, a banquet. He invited the councilors of the court, the generals of the army, and the governors of the lands. This feast was not just for one night, or two or three nights, or even ten nights. It went on for 180 nights.

When that big party ended, the king had another party just for the men of Susa where his royal palace was. He held it in the courtyard of the palace. The courtyard had big marble pillars. They were draped with fine blue cloth held in place with silver rings. The floor sparkled with mother-of-pearl and beautiful colored stones.

While the king was entertaining the men, Queen Vashti had a party for the women. It was in another part of the palace. I think they were far enough apart that one party didn't bother the other one.

On the seventh night of his party, the king was feeling pretty good and very important. He sent seven servants with a message for Queen Vashti.

The servants said to Queen Vashti, "A message from the king. 'Come to me. Wear your royal crown so all the men of Susa will see what a beautiful queen I have.'"

Queen Vashti thought for a moment. It was dangerous not to obey the king's command, but she was entertaining her own guests. She sent this message back to the king, "I will not come."

Was the king angry when he got her message! The more he thought about it, the angrier he got. "What must be done with Queen Vashti?" he asked the seven councilors of the court. They huddled together and whispered, "If the queen does not obey the king, our wives will find out, and they won't pay any attention to us. We cannot have that!" So they said to the king, "Send a royal decree to all the land. Say that because Queen Vashti did not obey your command to come to you, she is never able to come to you again; and get a new queen."

The king smiled. He liked that idea. In fact, the more he thought about it, the more he liked it. So a decree went out to all the land, from India to Ethiopia: "Because Queen Vashti refused to obey the king, she can never come before him again."

Now some people feel sorry for Vashti, but I think she was a brave and intelligent woman. Although she was no longer queen, she still lived in the palace, and I think she rather liked it that way.

❧ LECTIONARY DATES ❧

Paul and the Thessalonians
1 Thessalonians 3:9–13

When Paul entered a new city, he went first to the synagogue where the Jews gathered, and he told them about Jesus. If they weren't interested, he spoke in the homes of Gentiles, the people who weren't Jewish.

Not everyone wanted Paul to talk about Jesus. One time, when Paul was in Damascus, he learned that some Jewish leaders were plotting to kill him. His friends smuggled him out of town in a big basket that they lowered over the city wall after dark.

Paul and Silas, who often traveled with Paul, went to Thessalonica, where they taught about Jesus and started a church. The people there were good friends to Paul and Silas. Paul wanted to see them again, but he couldn't, so he sent his young friend Timothy to see how they were doing.

Timothy returned with a good report, but he mentioned that the Thessalonians needed some hope, some encouragement. Since Paul could not go to Thessalonica, he wrote a letter to the people in the church there.

This is part of what he wrote to the Thessalonians: "You have brought us so much joy before God. Each day I pray that I will see you again and will help you to continue to grow in faith. I hope that God will send us back to you. Now I pray that God will make your numbers grow and that your love for one another will be as full as our love for you. May God make your hearts strong and you holy until Jesus returns. Amen."

What do you think? Will these words give the Thessalonians hope in God?

Prayer: God, when we are upset, we can read Paul's words to the Thessalonians and remember that you will make us strong. Amen.

Who Is John?
Luke 3:1–6

Zechariah was a priest at the temple in Jerusalem. One day the angel Gabriel came to him and said, "Your wife Elizabeth will have a baby boy. You will name him John." Zechariah couldn't believe this was true because he and Elizabeth were very old, much too old to have a baby. Because Zechariah doubted the angel's message, he could not speak until after the baby was born.

When this surprising baby boy arrived, Elizabeth said, "We will name him John." Everyone was shocked to hear that the baby was not going to be named after his father. That was what usually happened. Zechariah still could not speak, so he wrote on a clay tablet: "His name is John."

This surprising baby boy grew up to be an even more surprising man. He lived in the desert wilderness until the word of God came to him. John had an important job to do. He was to get the people ready for the Messiah, the one God had promised to send.

John went to the Jordan River. He needed to be close to water because John's job was to baptize people. In those days, baptisms were in a river, not a building.

As people walked along the river, John called out, "Come! Tell God you are sorry for the wrong things you have done. Be baptized! Show God you want to change your heart and life."

When some people heard John, they remembered the words from the prophet Isaiah, spoken many years before:

> "Someone is shouting in the desert:
>   'Get the road ready for the Lord;
>   make a straight path for him to travel!
> Every valley must be filled up,
>   every hill and mountain leveled off.
> The winding roads must be made straight,
>   and the rough paths made smooth.
>   The whole human race will see God's salvation!'"
>
> (vv. 4–6 GNT)

All kinds of people came to John to be baptized in the Jordan River. They came to show God that they wanted to change their hearts and lives. So many heard about John that he was called John the baptizer.

Prayer: God, we hear John's message to live in your way. We want to do that too. Amen.

Tough Talk
Luke 3:7–18

People who were baptized by John told their friends, who told more people. Word spread about John the baptizer, that he could be found at the Jordan River. All kinds of people came to see him. Some came because they were sorry about how they lived, and some came because they were curious. Others came to be seen there so people would know how religious they were.

"John, baptize me," people called.

John looked at the crowd. "You snakes!" he shouted. "Did you come to be baptized so people would think well of you? Do you think being baptized is a game? Change your lives and then come to me. Do something good with the talents God has given you! Just because you claim Abraham as an ancestor, don't think you can come here. God expects good lives."

"What should we do?" asked some people.

"If you have two coats, give one coat to someone who doesn't have any coats. If you have plenty to eat, give food to someone who is hungry," John told them.

Some tax collectors in the crowd asked, "What should we do, John?"

John looked them in the eye. "Collect only as much money in taxes as is fair. Don't cheat people!"

Roman soldiers were standing on the edge of the crowd so trouble didn't start. One soldier asked, "What about us, John? What should we do?"

"Don't threaten or bully people. Be satisfied with the money you earn," answered John.

A man who had followed the crowd to the river asked, "Who is this man? He looks like a prophet. He sounds like a man from God."

A person near the man said, "Do you think he is God's Messiah, the Promised One?"

Overhearing the last question, John said, "I baptize with water, but one is coming who will baptize with God's Holy Spirit. He will make things right between God and you. He will get rid of sin forever."

When the people heard this, they wondered when this Promised One from God would come.

Prayer: God, during Advent we wait for the One that John said was coming. We get ready for the Promised One from God. Amen.

Two Babies
Luke 1:39–45 (46–55)

Before John the baptizer was born, the angel Gabriel came to Zechariah, his father, who was at work in the temple. Gabriel told Zechariah that his wife Elizabeth would have a baby boy. Zechariah didn't believe Gabriel because he and Elizabeth were much too old to have babies. Gabriel also told Zechariah that they were to name the baby John. Then they waited for their baby to be born.

Not long after Gabriel talked with Zechariah in the temple, Gabriel went to Nazareth looking for a young woman named Mary. When Gabriel found her, he said, "You are going to have a baby boy, a special baby boy. You are to name him Jesus."

Mary was shocked. The angel Gabriel also told Mary that her relative Elizabeth was going to have a baby.

Mary decided to visit Elizabeth so they could talk about their babies waiting to be born.

Mary had a long walk to the home of Zechariah and Elizabeth, which was in the hill country outside Jerusalem.

When she got close to the house, she called, "Elizabeth!" Elizabeth hurried to greet her.

Elizabeth was surprised to see Mary, but, of course, you couldn't phone or send an e-mail back then to say, "I'll see you in two weeks."

When Elizabeth heard Mary's voice, the baby inside Elizabeth jumped. At that moment, Elizabeth was filled with God's Spirit. She said to Mary, "God has blessed you above all women. Your baby is blessed. My baby jumped with joy inside me when I heard your voice."

Mary praised God with all her heart:
"God is great!
God is mighty!
We belong to God!
We can count on God to help us!"

Mary stayed with Elizabeth and Zechariah for three months. When it was almost time for Elizabeth's baby to be born, Mary went home to Nazareth.

Prayer: God, just as Mary and Elizabeth waited, we wait for the birth of a baby too: the Christ child. Amen.

A Child Is Born
Luke 2:1–20

When Mary returned to Nazareth after visiting Zechariah and Elizabeth, she and Joseph were to be married. Joseph belonged to the house and family of David, who was king many years ago.

When it almost time for Mary to have her baby, Caesar Augustus, the Roman emperor, sent out a decree, a law, that everyone in the Roman Empire was to sign up on the tax lists. To do that, Joseph and Mary had to go to Bethlehem, which was David's city.

When they got there, they discovered that the town was filled with other people of the house of David. They couldn't find any place to stay except a room where cattle slept. In this room, Mary's baby was born. She wrapped him in a blanket and laid him in a manger, where food for the cattle was placed.

That same night, some shepherds were in the field, taking care of their sheep, making sure no wild animals got them. Suddenly, the sky lit up and an angel from God stood right in front of them.

"Don't be afraid," said the angel. "I have good news for you. Your savior was born tonight in Bethlehem. Go into the town and find him. Look for a child wrapped in a blanket, sleeping in a manger."

As soon as the angel finished, hundreds, maybe thousands of angels in the sky sang, "Glory to God! Peace on earth!"

Then the angels left, and the shepherds said, "Let's go find this baby in a manger."

They ran to Bethlehem. There they found the baby sleeping in a manger and Mary and Joseph watching over him. When the shepherds left the stable, they told everyone they saw about this special baby, and everyone was amazed.

Prayer: God, today we celebrate the birth of Jesus, your son. What a happy day! Amen.

Where Is Jesus?
Luke 2:41–52

When Jesus was twelve years old, he traveled with Mary and Joseph to Jerusalem to celebrate the Passover festival. Jews from all over came to the city for this celebration of the exodus. This may have been Jesus' first trip to the royal city.

Along the way from Nazareth, they met other people going to Jerusalem. Sometimes they sang praises to God as they walked. When they got to Jerusalem, they gave offerings at the temple. They listened to the temple leaders read the Scriptures and teach about them.

When the festival of Passover ended, those who had traveled to the city left for home. The crowds leaving the city were large, and it was hard to keep track of people. Jesus wasn't with Mary and Joseph, but they thought he was walking with friends.

When it was nearly time to stop for the night, Mary and Joseph began to look for Jesus. "Have you seen Jesus?" they asked. No one had seen Jesus since they left Jerusalem that morning. Now his parents began to worry.

They hurried back to Jerusalem. For three days, they looked for Jesus. They went to the marketplace and the house where they had stayed. They looked everywhere they could. Then they went to the temple. Sure enough, Jesus was in the temple. He was talking with the Jewish leaders and teachers, who were asking him questions and looking amazed at what Jesus said.

"Jesus," interrupted Mary, "why did you do this? We have been searching for you for three days! Didn't you think we would be worried?"

Looking at them, Jesus said, "Didn't you know I would be in my Father's house?"

The teachers looked puzzled now.

Mary, Joseph, and Jesus began the long walk back to Nazareth. That long walk gave Mary a lot of time to think about what had happened and about Jesus' words. After that, Jesus obeyed Mary and Joseph and grew just as God had planned.

Prayer: God, as Jesus was in God's house, the temple, we are happy to be in God's house, our church, where we can praise you and learn about you. Amen.

Sent from God
John 1:(1–9) 10–18

Many years after Jesus lived on earth, a man named John, but not John the baptizer, wanted to tell people how special Jesus was. He didn't tell about visits from the angel Gabriel. He didn't tell about the visit of Mary and Elizabeth. He didn't tell about a baby born in a a room where animals stayed and angels announcing the birth to shepherds watching over their sheep. He didn't even tell about wise men from a land far away who came with expensive gifts.

John did something very different from those stories. John talked about Jesus coming to earth as the Word of God and as Light from God.

John's story is the fourth Gospel in our Bible. You know from the first words that his story is not like the others. John wrote that Jesus was with God from the very beginning of creation. John assured the people that when they believed that Jesus was from God, they became God's children. Imagine that, children of God!

John described Jesus not as a tiny baby but as one who was full of grace and truth. From Jesus, we—you and me—receive that grace, a love bigger than anything we can imagine.

No one has seen God, wrote John, but we know more about God through Jesus.

When John's Gospel was read to people, they thought and thought about who Jesus is. Today, when we read John's words, we think and think too. That is a good thing, because our thinking about Jesus brings us closer to God.

Prayer: God, thank you for sending Jesus so that we can know more about you. Amen.

From Afar
Matthew 2:1–12

Some wise men, also called magi, lived in a land far from Bethlehem. They studied the night sky, looking for new stars or other heavenly bodies. One night, they saw a bright star in the eastern sky that they had not seen before. "What could this mean?" one man asked.

"Surely this star is the sign of a new ruler in the East. Let's go find out for ourselves," said another.

Getting to the land in the East took many, many months. The wise men traveled with camels loaded with food and everything they needed for this long journey.

At last they arrived in Jerusalem, where King Herod was in charge. As travelers from another land, they knew it was a good idea to check in with the king, so they went to his palace.

When the wise men stood before King Herod, they asked, "Where is the new king of the Jews? We saw his star in the eastern sky and have come to give him gifts."

This news of a new king upset King Herod, but he didn't want the wise men to know that he was upset. So he consulted his advisors and asked them where this new king was to be born.

After the advisors talked together, they told the king, "In Bethlehem of Judea, according to the prophet of God."

King Herod returned to the wise men and cleverly found out when the star announcing the new king's birth had appeared in the sky. Then he said, "Go to Bethlehem and find this little king. When you return home, stop here and tell me where he is. I want to take gifts to him too."

The wise men left for Bethlehem that night so they could see and follow the star, which would mark the place where the little king was. They finally came to the house in Bethlehem where Mary, Joseph, and the child Jesus lived.

When they went in, they found Mary with Jesus. Then the wise men unpacked the camel with the gifts for the new king. They gave him gold and expensive materials: frankincense and myrrh. Before they left Bethlehem, the wise men had a dream. In it they were warned not to return to King Herod. So the wise men did not go to Jerusalem but went home by another way.

Prayer: God, we want to give gifts to honor the child Jesus too. Amen.

A Special Baptism
Luke 3:15–17, 21–22

Remember John the baptizer who baptized people in the Jordan River? John was the son of Zechariah and Elizabeth. Before John was born, his mother felt him jump when she heard Mary's voice calling to her.

John was known for preaching and baptizing people in the Jordan River. Some people thought John might be the one from God, the Messiah for whom they waited. But John said, "I baptize with water. The Messiah will baptize with the Holy Spirit. I am not good enough to untie the Messiah's sandals."

Every day John was at the Jordan River. People always knew they could find him there. One day, Jesus came and John baptized him too. While John was praying with Jesus, the sky opened and the Holy Spirit came down to Jesus in the shape of a bird, a dove.

But that wasn't all. A voice from above said, "You are my Son. I love you so much. You make me very happy."

Jesus was baptized when he was about thirty years old. What a special day and baptism that was!

Prayer: God, we know that you love us just as you loved Jesus. Thank you for your love. Amen.

The House Church in Corinth
1 Corinthians 12:1–11

The church in Corinth was begun by Paul on one of his trips to tell people about Jesus. The people in Corinth gathered in homes, perhaps outside in the courtyard when the weather was nice. They ate together. They prayed together. They sang praises to God together. But on this day, they had something special. A letter had come from Paul! You see, there had been some arguments in the church in Corinth, and no one seemed to know what to do. They hoped that Paul could help them. To remind the people that everyone was important to Jesus, this is what Paul wrote to the church in Corinth:

From Paul, an apostle of Jesus Christ, to the church in Corinth,

Brothers and sisters, I want you to know about gifts from the Holy Spirit. There are many different gifts, but all of them come from God's Holy Spirit. Each one of you has been given a gift to use for the good of everyone. One of you may have knowledge and can teach others about God. Or perhaps you have the gift of healing and can make people well. Whatever gift you have, it was given to you by God. Whatever gift you have, use it well.

That made everyone, young and old, think about their gifts. What did God want them to do? Even we, in this church today, ask that same question. How does God want us to use our gifts from the Holy Spirit?

Prayer: God, thank you for our gifts from the Holy Spirit. We will use them for the good of everyone. Amen.

Ezra Reads God's Law
Nehemiah 8:1–3, 5–6, 8–10

Long, long ago, an army from a country called Babylon invaded the land of Judah and destroyed the city of Jerusalem. Many Jewish people were forced to go live in Babylon. They lived in Babylon for about fifty years. Then a new king came to the throne. This king told the Jewish people that they could return to Jerusalem and rebuild the temple. This is what they did. The story of how that happened is in the book of Ezra in the Old Testament of our Bible.

When Nehemiah, who was still in Babylon, heard that the temple was rebuilt but that the city walls had not been repaired, he asked the king if he could go to Jerusalem and repair the city walls. The king appointed Nehemiah governor of the area and put him in charge of rebuilding the city walls. This was a huge job. There were many problems, but Nehemiah and the Jewish people kept at the work, and the walls were totally repaired in fifty-two days. Amazing!

Now that the temple and the city walls were repaired, Ezra, a prophet of God, had the job of teaching God's ways to the people. He called for everyone to gather in the city square by the Water Gate. Women and men, young and old, came. Ezra climbed up on a wooden platform. He had the scroll with the book of the Law of Moses on it. When Ezra opened the scroll, all the people sat down. Ezra read the scroll to the people from early morning until the middle of the afternoon. Everyone listened carefully, and all you could hear was Ezra's voice. When Ezra stopped reading, the people worshiped God.

Ezra had helpers as he taught the people. Teachers walked among the crowd to help the people understand the Law of Moses. Some people were so overjoyed at hearing these words that they cried.

"Don't cry," said Ezra and Nehemiah. "This day is holy. Go home and eat and drink. Also take food to people who have nothing to eat today. The joy of God is your strength."

The people did what they were told with great joy, because they had been taught God's law.

Prayer: God, we will follow your word, and we will take food to people who have nothing to eat. We will rejoice that you are our God. Amen.

Not Yet
Jeremiah 1:4–10

In the days long before Jesus, God spoke directly to people who became God's prophets. The messages given to
the prophets were for God's people. And God's people didn't
always want to hear that message from God.

The people God chose to be prophets were usually a surprise. They were not the best preachers; they were not the
most honored family members. To hear that God wanted you
to be a prophet was both scary and exciting. This is how one
prophet, Jeremiah, wrote about the day God called him to be
a prophet:

God said to me, "Before you were born, I chose you. I
chose you to be a prophet to the nations."

But I said, "God, I don't know how to speak to nations. I
am only a child."

"Don't say you are only a child," God said. "Where I tell
you to go, you will go. What I tell you to say, you will say.
Don't be afraid of anyone, because I will be with you to take
care of you."

Then God stretched out a hand and touched my mouth.
"I'm putting my words into your mouth. Today, right now,

I give you power over nations to dig up and tear down, to destroy and flatten, to build and to plant."

Jeremiah was God's prophet for many years. The book with his name in the Old Testament is one of the longest books about prophets. He had some rough times, but Jeremiah was always faithful to God.

Prayer: God, we want to be faithful to you as Jeremiah was faithful. Amen.

Fishing with Jesus
Luke 5:1–11

On a bright, sunny day, Jesus was at the edge of Lake Gennesaret, also called the Sea of Galilee, when people began to arrive—lots of people. There were so many people that Jesus was being backed up into the water. They were eager to hear Jesus teach about God.

Two fishing boats were at the edge of the water. The owners had been out fishing and were now back, washing their nets so they would be ready for the next night of fishing.

Jesus got into one of the boats, one that belonged to Simon, who was also called Peter.

"Would you row me out just a bit from the shore?" Jesus asked.

When Simon did, Jesus sat down in the boat and began to teach the people. He taught them about God's love and care.

When he was finished, he turned to Simon and said, "Row out into the deep water and let down your nets so you can catch fish."

Now Simon had just come ashore after a long night of fishing and not catching one fish.

He said, "Master, we have been out all night and we didn't

catch even one tiny fish. However, if you insist, I will drop my nets here."

Even though it was clear to Simon that Jesus didn't know anything about fishing, there was something exciting about this man and his teaching. Simon and his crew let the nets down into the deep water. Before they could blink an eye, their nets were so full they could barely pull all the fish into the boat. The nets were so full of fish they had to call for help from the other boat. Even then, both boats were so loaded down that they were about to sink. What a lot of fish!

When Simon saw this incredible catch of fish, he fell to his knees before Jesus and said, "Go away, for I am no good."

"Simon," Jesus said, "don't be afraid. From now on, you will be catching people, not fish."

James and John, Zebedee's sons, who were Simon's fishing partners, also saw this gigantic catch of fish, and they were amazed.

As soon as the two boats loaded with fish got to the shore, Simon, James, and John left everything behind and went with Jesus.

Prayer: God, we will listen to Jesus' teaching and follow him too, with your help. Amen.

Be Happy
Luke 6:17–26

After the day that Jesus asked Simon, James, and John to go with him, he chose nine more men, including Simon's brother Andrew, to be his disciples, people who would stay with him day after day, month after month, and year after year.

More and more people heard about Jesus. He couldn't go anywhere without a crowd gathering around him. One time he went up on a mountain where he prayed all night. When he came down from the mountain to a large flat piece of land, a big crowd from all over the countryside came. They wanted to hear him teach, and they wanted him to heal them.

He looked to the side where his disciples were standing, and said:

"If you are poor, be happy because all that is God's
  is yours.
"If you are hungry, be happy because you will have
  all you need to be full.
"If you are sad and crying, be happy because you
  will laugh.

"If people make fun of you because you follow me, be happy and jump for joy for you have a great prize waiting for you in heaven."

Jesus taught the crowd for a long time that day. Jesus' words made the people think about God and God's love for them. We still think about these words and what they mean for us. Next week you'll hear some more of what he told them.

Prayer: God, we are happy to learn what Jesus taught. Amen.

A New Kind of Love
Luke 6:27–38

A crowd of men, women, and children stood around Jesus as he taught. After a while, some of them sat on the ground, especially the children. Imagine that you are there with your family. You have heard the adults around you talking about this teacher, this rabbi, Jesus and the way that he teaches. You were excited when your parents said you were going to hear him today. It was a long walk, but it was fun to walk with your friends. Sometimes you sang songs of praise to God.

But really, some of what this Jesus said doesn't make much sense to you. So you watch birds flying overhead and think about other things. Then Jesus says: "Listen if you are ready to hear. Love your enemies. Do good to people who do bad things to you. Pray for people who are mean to you. If someone slaps you on your cheek, turn the other cheek so it can be hit too."

Goodness, you wonder, does Jesus really mean this is how God wants us to live? But Jesus had more to say, "Treat people the same way that you want them to treat you. Love your enemies. Do good to everyone. If you do, you will be doing what God wants you to do and following the way that God treats you."

Love your enemy or love anyone who is mean to you. Did Jesus really mean you?

Prayer: God, thank you for loving us and showing us how to love others. Amen.

A Strong Foundation
Luke 6:39–49

The people listened carefully to Jesus. He had much to teach them as they sat on a flat stretch of land one day. Jesus promised that people who were hungry or poor or sad would be made happy. He told the crowd to love their enemies and do good things for people who were mean to them. He taught them to treat people as you want them to treat you.

Just before he stopped that day, Jesus told the crowd a story. Jesus was a very good storyteller, and his stories gave everyone lots to think about. So after Jesus had taught the crowd all about how to live in the way God wanted them to live, he told this story:

"When you come to hear me teach, and then you do what I tell you, it is like this: When you are building a house, you dig down deep so you can build on a solid foundation. Then when the storms come, your house will not be destroyed because you built it the right way. Now when you come to hear me teach but you don't do what I tell you, it is like this: When you are building a house, you don't bother with a solid foundation at all. Then when the storm comes and the town is flooded, your house is washed away."

As the people thought about this story, they wondered what kind of building they were and whether or not they had strong foundations based in God's love. Meanwhile, Jesus and the disciples went to the next town.

Prayer: God, help us build strong foundations to live your way. Amen.

A Changed Saul
Acts 9:1–20*

Saul had permission from the high priest to go to Damascus to hunt for people, Jews, who were followers of Jesus. Saul was certain that Jesus was wrong and that his followers were dangerous, and Saul wanted them to be punished.

Saul and his traveling companions started off to Damascus on horseback. When they were near Damascus, a bright light came around Saul, and he fell off his horse. Saul heard a voice saying, "Saul, Saul, why do you treat me so badly?"

"Who are you?" asked Saul.

"I am Jesus. When you hurt my followers, you hurt me. Get up and go into Damascus. Then you will be told what to do."

The men with Saul were shocked and frightened. They heard the voice, but they couldn't see anyone. They helped Saul up, but when he opened his eyes, he couldn't see. So the men had to take him by the hand and walk with him into Damascus.

They settled him in a room and left him. For three days, he was there without water or food and unable to see.

*Galatians 1:1–12 is the lectionary text, but the story is based on Acts 9:1–20 since Paul refers to this experience immediately following the lectionary text.

Now in this city lived a follower of Jesus named Ananias. Jesus spoke to Ananias in a dream. "Go to Straight Street and ask for a man named Saul, who is from Tarsus. In a dream, he has seen you enter and place your hands on him so he can see again."

"My Lord," exclaimed Ananias, "I have heard of this Saul of Tarsus. He wants to jail and hurt your followers. He has permission to arrest us and take us back to Jerusalem."

"Go to this man now!" said Jesus, "I have chosen him to take my story to all people."

Ananias went to the house on Straight Street. He placed his hands on Saul, and something that looked like scales fell from Saul's eyes so he could see again. Ananias baptized Saul and gave him food.

Saul stayed with the followers of Jesus in Damascus for several days. He immediately began to preach about Jesus, God's Son, in the synagogue. Everyone was surprised!

Prayer: God, we are surprised about Saul's change, but now we know that you can use anyone to tell the story of Jesus; us too. Amen.

An Awesome Experience
Luke 9:28–36 (37–43)

When Jesus began to travel around the countryside teaching and healing people, he chose twelve disciples to travel with him. He wanted them to learn to do what he was doing. They listened to him teach the crowds. They watched him heal people who were sick. Where Jesus went, they went.

One sunny day, Jesus asked three of the disciples—Peter (also called Simon), James, and John—to go with him up a mountain to pray. Jesus often went up a mountain to pray, so they weren't surprised when he invited them to go with him. It was quieter on the mountain than on the flat plain where people would find him easily.

They talked a bit as they walked. They watched the clouds glide across the sky. Finally, they came to a flat place near the top of the mountain, a good place to sit and pray to God. Peter, James, and John might have been thinking about the beautiful world God created or how wonderful it was to be with Jesus every day.

The combination of the warm sunshine and the walk up the mountain made the men a little sleepy. Their eyes were closing when suddenly Jesus changed. Jesus' face looked different, but they weren't sure why. His clothes sparkled like sun on the lake or a lightning flash in the night sky.

Then, from nowhere, Moses and Elijah, two of God's prophets from long ago, were standing beside Jesus.

"Jesus, I will make monuments for you and Moses and Elijah," said Peter. But before he could finish his sentence, a cloud came over the place. The disciples were filled with wonder and awe.

"This is my Son, the one I have chosen. Listen to him!" said a voice from high in the cloud.

When the cloud lifted, Moses and Elijah were gone. Peter, James, and John couldn't say a word, and they didn't tell anyone what they had seen when they went down the mountain.

Prayer: God, we want to listen to Jesus too. Amen.

Forty Days in the Desert Wilderness
Luke 4:1–13

On Ash Wednesday, which was last Wednesday, the church entered the season of Lent, the weeks that lead to Easter. The stories during Lent help the church understand who Jesus is.

A few weeks ago, not long after Christmas, the Bible story was about when John the baptizer baptized Jesus in the Jordan River. On that day, Jesus was filled with the Holy Spirit. That Spirit led Jesus into the desert wilderness, which is a land where there are mostly rocks and very few plants.

Jesus went there to pray and fast, which means that he didn't eat anything. He had been in this desert wilderness with no food for forty days, which is longer than a month. He was so hungry, not like when you want a snack. Jesus was starving, really!

Then the devil, the one who tempts us to do wrong, came to Jesus. "Since you are God's Son, change these stones into bread."

"No," said Jesus, "it is written in the Scriptures that people do not live by bread alone."

Then the tempter took Jesus to a high place where they could see all the lands of the world. "If you will worship me and not God," said the tempter, "I will make you ruler over all that you see."

"No," said Jesus, "it is written in the Scriptures to worship God and only God."

But the tempter wasn't ready to give up. This time, the tempter took Jesus to Jerusalem, to the highest part of the temple. "If you believe so much in God, jump from this high place, and God will send angels to save you so you won't be hurt."

"No," said Jesus, "it is written in the Scriptures not to test God."

Then the tempter left Jesus, but the tempter kept thinking about other ways to get Jesus to do wrong.

Prayer: God, let Jesus be an example for us when we are tempted to do something wrong. Amen.

A Warning from Pharisees
Luke 13:31–35

Jesus and the disciples had been traveling around the countryside of Galilee for a long time. Sometimes people traveled with them for a few days and then went home. At other times, large crowds came to hear Jesus preach and teach or they brought people who were sick to be healed.

The whole time, according to the writer of Luke, Jesus planned to go to Jerusalem. Jesus was intent on ending up in Jerusalem. Now they were just outside the city walls.

Perhaps they were resting in the shade of a tree, looking toward the city, when some Pharisees came to Jesus. Pharisees were Jewish leaders who believed that following the Law of Moses to the very smallest command was the most important thing to do. Sometimes Pharisees tried to trick Jesus with their difficult questions. But not this time. This time, they said to Jesus, "Go away from Jerusalem. Herod wants to kill you."

"Tell that sly fox Herod that I will be teaching and healing for three days, and then I'll come into the city," said Jesus.

Jesus looked to the city. "Jerusalem, Jerusalem, you kill God's prophets. So many times I have wanted to gather you safely like a hen gathers her chicks under her wings when danger is near. But you wouldn't stand for that. Now it is too late. You won't recognize me until you say, 'Bless the one who comes in the name of God.'"

Then Jesus went about his work, teaching about God's love and healing people who were sick.

Prayer: God, be with us during these days of Lent so that we will find safety in you. Amen.

A Message of Hope
Isaiah 55:1–9

The prophet of God named Isaiah, whose story is told in the Old Testament or Hebrew Scriptures, is quoted many times in the Gospels, where the story of Jesus is told. When Jesus read in the synagogue, he read from the scroll of Isaiah. This story is about a message from God that Isaiah had for God's people.

Jerusalem had been attacked and defeated by the Babylonian soldiers. Many of the people of Jerusalem were captured and forced to live in Babylon. After some years, life became normal for them there, but, and this is big, they were forgetting how to live as God's people.

But Isaiah was in Babylon and, being a prophet of God, Isaiah had not forgotten how to live as God's people. And Isaiah had a message of hope from God to give to the people.

Isaiah gathered the people from Jerusalem together and told them,

> "Listen! This is what God says to you!
> "If you are thirsty, come to the water!
> "If you are hungry, but you have no money,
>   come and get food to eat!

"Don't spend money on food that doesn't fill
   you up.
"Listen carefully. Eat what is good.
"God will make a covenant, a promise, with you
   that will last forever!
"Seek God where God can still be found. Call for
   God.
"Return to God because God is generous and will
   forgive you.
"Like the heavens are high above the earth, God's
   ways are high above the ways of humans."

The people listened carefully. They remembered the loving God who was their God. Their hearts were filled with
hope that God was still with them.

Prayer: God, Isaiah reminds us that you are with us. We will
take that hope with us today. Amen.

Two Sons
Luke 15:1–3, 11b–32

The story today may be the most famous story that Jesus ever told. Jesus told this story to some people who complained that Jesus welcomed everyone and even ate meals with people who others thought were bad people.

"A man had two sons. One day the younger son came to the father and said, 'Father, I would like my share of the inheritance now.' The father divided up the inheritance between the two sons. Then the younger son went to another country. In this other country, he lived the good life and made friends immediately.

"But when his money ran out, the friends were nowhere to be found, and the younger son was in trouble. At the same time, there was not enough food for everyone in this country, which made life even more difficult for the younger son. He went to work for a farmer, who sent him into the fields to feed the pigs. Even the food for the pigs, which is called *slop*, looked pretty good to this younger son. No one gave the younger son any food, not even slop.

"One day as the younger son was feeding the pigs, he said to himself, 'What am I doing? My father's workers have more to eat than I do here. I will go to my father, ask him to forgive

44

me, and ask to be one of his workers.' The younger son left immediately for his home.

"Long before the younger son got there, his father saw him coming. He ran to meet his son and hugged and kissed him.

"'Father,' said the younger son, 'I have done wrong against you and against heaven. I don't deserve to be your son.'

"But it was almost as if the father didn't hear him, because he called to a servant, 'Get the best robe and put it on my son. Put rings on his fingers and sandals on his feet! Cook a feast, for we are going to celebrate. This son who was lost is home again!'

"All the servants were busy preparing this excellent feast when the older son returned from a hard day's work. 'What's going on?' he asked.

"'Your brother has come back, and your father has ordered a feast to celebrate,' answered a servant rushing by.

"'What? I'll have nothing to do with any of this celebration,' said the older son.

"When the father realized what was going on, he went to the older son and said, 'Please, please, come to the celebration feast.'

"'I have worked every day for you,' said the older son. 'You have never given a feast for me. But my brother who went off returns broke, and you throw a party for him!'

"'My son,' said the father, 'you are with me every day, and everything I have is yours. Today we celebrate because your brother, who was lost, is found.'"

I wonder what the people who complained that Jesus ate with everyone thought about this story.

Prayer: God, we know that your love for us is bigger and deeper than we can imagine. Thank you. Amen.

Expensive Perfume
John 12:1–8

Besides the twelve disciples who traveled with Jesus, Jesus had three good friends who lived in a small village named Bethany, a little way outside Jerusalem. The friends were two sisters, Mary and Martha, and their brother Lazarus. Jesus and the disciples stopped in Bethany to visit the three. Feeding that many people was a real job. Martha served the meal. Lazarus sat and talked with Jesus and the disciples. But Mary did something unusual.

Jesus, Lazarus, and the disciples were ready to eat. Martha was bringing in the food. Then Mary walked to Jesus, carrying a jar of perfume, very expensive perfume. She knelt down and wiped it on his feet. Then she bowed her head and wiped his feet dry with her long hair.

The sweet scent of the perfume filled the house. Judas Iscariot, one of the disciples, was upset, "That perfume cost a lot of money. Why wasn't that money spent on people who are poor and hungry? This is a waste!"

Jesus turned to Judas and said, "Leave her alone. She can use this perfume as she wishes. You will always have people who are poor around you, but you won't always have me."

Judas looked away, not sure what to say or do next. But Mary probably smiled.

Prayer: God, teach us to celebrate that Jesus is with us. Amen.

Without the Palm Branches
Luke 19:28–40

The story of Jesus' arrival in Jerusalem for Passover is in all four Gospels: Matthew, Mark, Luke, and John. This is how it is told in the Gospel of Luke.

Jesus and the disciples were on their way to Jerusalem. When they got close, as close as the neighboring villages of Bethpage and Bethany on the Mount of Olives, they stopped.

Jesus called two disciples aside and gave them a job. "Go to the village," he said, pointing to a nearby settlement. "Right away you will see a colt tied to a post. No one has ever ridden this colt. Bring it to me. If anyone asks you what you are doing, say, 'Its master wants it.'"

The two disciples did what Jesus said. As they were untying the colt, someone came over and said, "What are you doing?" They answered, "Its master wants it."

They brought the colt to Jesus. Then some of them threw their cloaks over its back and helped Jesus up on the back of the colt.

Off they went to Jerusalem. As they walked in front of Jesus, who was riding the colt, the disciples spread their cloaks on the road. When they started down the hill from the Mount of Olives, many more disciples shouted joyfully. They praised God for all God's good work. They also said, "Bless the king who comes in the name of God! Peace in heaven and glory in the highest heaven!"

Some Pharisees in the crowd heard the people praising God and shouting about a king. They said to Jesus, "Make them be quiet! This talk about a king will get everyone in trouble."

But Jesus said, "If they are quiet, these stones on the road would shout."

Prayer: God, today we join the people who welcomed Jesus to Jerusalem. We are glad to worship you. Amen.

A Silly Story?
Luke 24:1–12

Jesus died on Friday. Mary Magdalene, Joanna, and Mary the mother of James, who watched him die, followed his body to the tomb. They saw a huge stone rolled in front of the burial cave. Then they left to prepare spices and salves to spread over Jesus' body. This was the custom when someone died. But the next day was the Sabbath, when they did no work according to God's law, so they waited until the third day to return to the tomb.

On that day, the three women, Mary Magdalene, Joanna, and Mary the mother of James, got up as soon as the sun appeared in the sky. They took the spices and salves to the tomb to spread over Jesus' body.

They walked quietly and silently. One of them probably wondered how they were going to move that big stone that covered the doorway.

But when they got to the tomb, they were shocked to find that someone had already rolled the huge stone away. They could walk right into the tomb. And when they did, the body of Jesus wasn't there!

What they did see were two men dressed in dazzling, blinding white clothes. The women were frightened and turned their faces away from the men.

"Why are you looking for Jesus here? Remember, Jesus told you that he would die and then rise on the third day."

Of course, they remembered! They went back to where the other disciples were staying and told them what had happened. But the disciples looked at them blankly. What silly stories these women tell!

However, Peter also remembered what Jesus told them, and he wasn't so sure this was a silly story. He ran to the tomb to see for himself. When he looked in, he saw only the linen cloths in which Jesus had been wrapped. He walked back slowly, wondering what had happened.

Prayer: God, we are happy that we know the rest of the story of Jesus' resurrection. Thanks be to God. Amen.

Believe
John 20:19–31

On the same day that three women—Mary Magdalene, Joanna, and Mary the mother of James—went to the tomb and saw that it was empty, the other followers of Jesus were hiding in a house with the door locked. They were worried about the Roman soldiers and the Jewish leaders, who might be searching for them.

As they sat, not talking, Jesus suddenly was standing in front of them, but no one had opened the door, which was still locked.

"Peace be with you," said Jesus. No one said a word. Was this really Jesus, or were they dreaming?

Then Jesus showed them the wounds on his hands and his side. Yes, this had to be Jesus!

Now they were all speaking, they were so filled with joy.

"Peace be with you," Jesus said again. "As God sent me, I am sending you."

With that, he breathed on them and said, "Receive the Holy Spirit. Anyone you forgive, their sins will be forgiven."

Thomas, one of the disciples, was not in the room when Jesus was there. When he returned, everyone rushed to tell him what had happened.

"Unless I see the marks on his hands and side for myself, I won't believe that you saw him," said Thomas.

Eight days later, everyone, including Thomas, was in the house. Again Jesus stood before them, even though the door was locked.

"Peace be with you," Jesus said. "Thomas, put your finger here. Look at my hands. Believe!"

"My Lord and my God!" said Thomas, because he did believe.

"Do you believe because you see me?" asked Jesus. "Happy are those who do not see me but they believe."

The writer of the Gospel of John included this story so that we, who do not see Jesus, will believe.

Prayer: God, we give thanks for the stories about Jesus in our Bible so that we can believe. Amen.

Jesus Cooks Breakfast
John 21:1–19

On another day after Jesus' resurrection, the day we call Easter, Jesus appeared to the disciples. It happened on the shore of the Sea of Tiberias, also called the Sea of Galilee.

Many of the disciples were together when Simon Peter said, "I'm going fishing." He was a fisherman and felt most at home on the water.

Everyone else said, "I'll go too." The whole crew set off in a boat. It was evening, and they stayed out on the water and fished all night. But they didn't catch one fish.

Early in the morning, just as the sun was coming up, Jesus stood on the shore of the sea, but the disciples in the boat didn't know who he was.

When they got closer, Jesus yelled, "Have you caught anything to eat?"

"No," they shouted back.

"Throw your net over the right side of the boat and you'll find fish," Jesus said.

They threw their net over the right side of the boat and there were so many fish in it that they, all of them, could barely pull the catch of fish into the boat.

"It's the Lord Jesus," said a disciple.

When Simon Peter saw who it was, he jumped into the sea. The rest of the disciples stayed in the boat, dragging the net filled with fish. Fortunately they weren't very far from the shore, only about the length of a football field.

Jesus had a fire ready when they got there. He had already cooked fish on it, and he gave them bread.

"Bring some of the fish you caught," Jesus said.

Simon Peter pulled the net to the shore. It had one hundred fifty-three large fish in it. But even with all that fish, the net was not torn or damaged.

Then Jesus said, "Come. Have some breakfast."

Additional Ending for a Communion Sunday

Jesus doesn't cook breakfast for us today, but Jesus does invite us to eat together at the Communion table. Remember this story and Jesus' invitation to come and eat when we celebrate the Lord's Supper.

Prayer: God, we are thankful that Jesus fills us with stories and with his love. Amen.

Tabitha aka Dorcas

Acts 9:36–43

After Jesus left the apostles to do his work on earth, Peter traveled to other places telling about Jesus Christ. He taught and healed, just as Jesus did. At the beginning of our story, Peter is in Lydda.

In a city not too far away called Joppa was a woman who was a follower of Jesus. Her name was Tabitha, and she was also known as Dorcas. She did so many kind acts that people couldn't remember them all. She was known throughout the city as a woman who took care of others.

Then Dorcas got sick, so sick that she died. As was the custom, the women washed her body. This all happened in an upstairs room.

Since Lydda wasn't very far from Joppa, two of Dorcas's friends in Joppa went to Lydda because they heard that Peter was there and that he was healing people. They were to bring him to Dorcas in Joppa. "Please hurry and come with us!" they said to Peter.

As soon as Peter got to Joppa, Dorcas's friends took him upstairs to where she was. All the widows were crying and showing Peter the clothes Dorcas had made for others.

"Everyone," said Peter with a strong voice, "leave this room."

When they were gone, Peter knelt by Dorcas and prayed. Then he stood and said, "Tabitha, get up!" Peter reached out his hand, and Dorcas, also known as Tabitha, stood up.

Peter called downstairs for all the people to come. When they did, he pointed to Dorcas, who was standing beside him smiling. When the news about Dorcas got around Joppa, the people wanted Peter to stay there for a while, and he did.

Prayer: God, we give thanks for people like Dorcas who care for others. We want to follow in her path. Amen.

Two Visions
Acts 11:1–18

While Peter was still in Joppa, some men came to him with a message from Cornelius, a Roman soldier in Caesarea. "Our master had a vision from God, and in that vision he was told to send for you to come to him," they told Peter.

Peter also had a vision from God. In that vision, he saw a large sheet come down from the sky. In the sheet were all kinds of animals that Jews were not supposed to eat, according to God's law. But a voice told Peter to eat. Peter refused. "I cannot eat what God has said we should not eat." This happened three times. Then the voice said, "Peter, what God has made clean is no longer unclean." So when the men came from Cornelius, Peter and some other followers of Jesus went to Caesarea to see a man who was not Jewish.

When Peter and others got to Cornelius's house, they were welcomed warmly. Peter taught everyone in the house about Jesus. Then it was clear that the Holy Spirit had come to Cornelius and everyone in his household. The Jesus believers with Peter were amazed. Peter asked, "Can anyone say that these people should not be baptized?"

So Cornelius and everyone in his house were baptized in the name of Jesus Christ. Cornelius invited Peter to stay with them for several more days.

Meanwhile, in Jerusalem, some of the church leaders heard what had happened in Caesarea; they weren't sure this was a good thing. They were particularly concerned that Peter and the others had stayed in Cornelius's house and eaten there. Eating with people who weren't Jews was forbidden by the laws of Moses.

So Peter returned to Jerusalem and told the church leaders just what I have told you, about the visions and how the Holy Spirit came upon Cornelius and everyone who lived in his house. Then the church leaders stopped complaining and praised God for these new believers.

Prayer: God, from the story of Peter and Cornelius, we learn that you love everyone. We will try to do that too. Amen.

A New Friend, a New Church
Acts 16:9–15

Paul and Timothy, who had joined Paul in Lystra, were traveling together. One night, Paul had a vision. He saw a man from Macedonia, a land far from Jerusalem. This man pleaded, "Come to Macedonia. Help us."

Immediately Paul and Timothy set off for Macedonia. They took a ship to a place called Troas, and the next day they went to Neapolis. From there they traveled to Philippi, the most important city of Macedonia. This land was also under the rule of the Roman Empire.

The travelers stayed there for several days. On the Sabbath, the day for resting and praising God, Paul and the others went to the river, to a particular city gate, where they had heard people gathered to pray.

They sat down and spoke to the women who were there, telling them about Jesus Christ and God. One woman, a believer in God but not a Jew, was named Lydia. She was from a city called Thyatira, and she was a business woman who sold purple cloth, which was really expensive. In fact, Lydia was probably rich. She listened carefully to what Paul said and took it into her heart. Lydia and all who lived in her house were baptized that day. Then she invited Paul and the men traveling with him to stay at her house. And they stayed with her until they left Philippi.

Lydia was a good friend to Paul. The people in Philippi, who became a church, were some of Paul's best friends.

Prayer: God, we marvel at the way the good news of Jesus spread to many countries. We want to tell others too. Amen.

A Jailer Believes

Acts 16:16–34

While Paul and his friends were in Philippi, they went to a place of prayer each day. This was in a time when people had slaves. When they walked through the market-place, a slave girl shouted at them, "These men are slaves of the Most High God." This happened day after day. Finally, Paul had had enough.

This slave girl told the fortunes of people, who paid her owners. Paul shouted, "Spirit, I order you to come out of her." The spirit did, and the slave girl couldn't tell fortunes anymore. Her owners were furious!

They dragged Paul and Silas before the men of law. They claimed, "These men are Jews and are disturbing our peace." The men of law ordered Paul and Silas beaten and thrown into prison. They were put into a cell way in the back of the prison, and their legs were chained to the wall.

Paul and Silas spent the night singing songs and praising God. Suddenly an earthquake shook the walls so hard that the prison doors opened and the chains fell off their legs.

The jailer came to check on the prisoners because he was afraid that they had escaped. If they did, he would be in big trouble with the men of law.

"We are all here," shouted Paul to the jailer. The jailer brought the two men outside. "What must I do to be saved?" he asked.

"Believe in Christ Jesus, and you and everyone in your house will be saved," answered Paul. Then they told the jailer all about Jesus and God.

That very night, after the jailer had washed and wrapped the wounds of Paul and Silas, the jailer and everyone who lived in his house were baptized. Then everyone ate together, and the whole household was happy that the jailer now believed in Jesus.

Prayer: God, the stories of Paul's faithfulness are amazing. We want a faith like his. Amen.

Thousands of New Believers
Acts 2:1–21

For the last few weeks, the stories have been about Peter and others who spread the word about Jesus Christ to places outside Jerusalem. This story tells how the apostles received the power to do that.

Before Jesus went to be with God, he told his followers to wait in Jerusalem until they received the power of the Holy Spirit. Then they were to tell everyone, in every land, about Jesus Christ.

So they did. The Bible doesn't say how many days they had to wait, but it was quite a while, because the Holy Spirit came to them on the day of Pentecost, an important festival in the Jewish year. *Pentecost* means fiftieth day.

On this day of Pentecost, Jesus' disciples were all together in one room. Suddenly a sound like a tornado came rushing through the room. The sound filled every inch of the space. You couldn't get away from it. But no one was hurt, and nothing was disturbed.

Then flames of fire like tongues danced over each person's head, but no one was burned. Each person began to speak in a language that they couldn't speak before this moment.

Because it was Pentecost, Jews from many countries were

in Jerusalem, and the noise of the people speaking could be heard in the street. They were surprised to hear people not from their countries speaking their language. They crowded around the door and asked, "Aren't these people from Galilee? How can they speak languages from other countries, languages that we speak? We can hear them talking about God's power in our languages."

They looked at one another and asked, "What does this mean?"

Others laughed at the question and said, "They are drunk."

Peter heard them and said, "It is only eleven o'clock in the morning. We are not drunk!"

Then Peter went on to tell the people about Jesus Christ and God, because he now had the power of the Holy Spirit.

Some who heard Peter said, "What should we do?"

"Tell God you are sorry and will change, and then be baptized," answered Peter. "This promise of God's love is for you, for your children, and for your children's children."

The people who understood what Peter was telling them were baptized, about three thousand of them.

Prayer: God, we thank you that your Holy Spirit is among us today too. Amen.

The Glory of God
Psalm 8

If you open the Bible to the middle, you will probably be at the book called Psalms in the Old Testament. This is the longest book in the Bible, with one hundred fifty chapters, or psalms. The psalms are songs or prayers to God. We don't know who wrote them. Sometimes we sing them as joyful praise to God. Sometimes we read them as prayers when everything seems to be going wrong or we are very sad. The psalm for this Sunday is one that we might sing or read to give thanks and praise to God.

Although we don't know who wrote it, I like to think that a shepherd was out in the field with a flock of sheep or goats. Late one night, this shepherd looked up at the sky. How bright the stars were! How still everything was! The mountains could barely be seen in the distance. The moon was just bright enough to see that the sheep were safe. Maybe, just maybe, on a night like this, Psalm 8 was written. Listen to it and see what you think.*

God, our God,
Your name is found everywhere on earth!

*Instead of this paraphrase, you can read Psalm 8 in a contemporary language translation.

Your glory can be seen high above the heavens.
From the praise of children, you have built a safe
    place.
When I look up at the skies,
    at all that you made,
    the moon and the stars high above—
    what are human beings that you should care for
    us?
We are only a bit below all that is holy
    but you have asked us to rule
    over all that you created.
You have put everything at our feet.
    the sheep and the cattle,
    the wild animals too,
    birds in the sky and fish in the sea.
God, our God,
Your name is found everywhere on earth!

I wonder what you will say to God the next time you look up at the night sky.

Prayer: God, your creation fills us with wonder. We praise you. Amen.

Think about What You Do

Luke 6:39–49

Jesus asked disciples, followers, to travel with him so he could teach them about living God's way. On this day, he said to them, "Love the people who hate you or who are mean to you. Forgive them."

Surely some of the disciples didn't want to hear those words. How could they love someone who treated them badly? How could they forgive people who were mean to them and didn't even say they were sorry?

Then Jesus said more to his followers, "You know that a blind person can't lead another blind person, especially in a strange place, right? When you don't see the things you do wrong but you still complain about someone else doing those things, you are like a blind person leading another blind person. When you see clearly how to change the way you live, then you can help someone else."

Maybe this is what Jesus means. When you are upset because someone is teasing you, you probably tell your mother or father or a teacher. But you forget that yesterday or maybe an hour ago you were teasing that same person or someone else. Jesus wants us to think about what we do and change our ways before we try to help someone else change.

Prayer: God, help us look at how we act so that we can live as you want us to live. Amen.

(Sunday between May 29 and June 4 inclusive)

A Contest
1 Kings 18:20–21 (22–29), 30–39*

King Ahab called all the Israelites together at Mount Carmel as Elijah, the prophet of God, commanded him. The prophets of Baal were there too. Elijah stood in front of the Israelites and said, "Why do you go back and forth between our God and the god Baal? Make up your minds. Choose the one God, the Lord God!" The people didn't say a word.

Elijah said, "I am the last prophet of the Lord God here. Baal has three hundred and fifty prophets. Let's find out which God is the strongest. Bring your sacrifice. King Ahab's prophets will call on Baal; I will call on the Lord God. Whoever answers with fire is indeed God." Everyone said, "Yes, let's do it!"

Turning to the prophets of Baal, Elijah said, "There are so many of you. You start. Get your sacrifice ready and call on your god, but don't set fire to your sacrifice. Let Baal bring the fire."

---

*During Ordinary Time, the Revised Common Lectionary offers two Old Testament tracks. Some churches and denominations prefer the semi-continuous track and others use the track that compliments the Gospel reading. The OT texts used in this resource are from the semi-continuous track.

The prophets of Baal did as Elijah said. From morning until noon, they called on Baal to light the fire. At noon, Elijah laughed at them. "Cry louder! Surely Baal is thinking about something else. Or maybe he is asleep and you must wake him up!"

Indeed, the prophets of Baal continued to shout, louder than before. All day they danced and shouted to Baal. Still nothing happened.

The people stood watching all day. Elijah said to them, "Come closer." They came closer and watched as he built a new altar to the Lord God because the old one had been torn down. Then he dug a deep ditch around the altar. He stacked the wood on the altar. "Fill four big jars with water and pour it over the altar," Elijah ordered. "Then do it again! And do it a third time!"

After the third time, water had filled the ditch around the altar. By now it was evening. Elijah came to the altar and prayed, "Lord God of Abraham, Isaac, and Israel, you are God in Israel, and I am your servant. I have done all these things at your request. Answer me, Lord, so these people will know that you are God and you will welcome your people back to you."

In the wink of an eye, fire fell from the sky and burned the wood, the offering, the stones, and the dust. It even dried up all the water in the ditch around the altar. When the Israelites saw this, they fell to the ground, saying, "The Lord is the real God! The Lord is the real God!"

Prayer: God, you are the real God. We are happy to be your people. Amen.

(Sunday between June 5 and June 11 inclusive)

A Man of God
1 Kings 17:8–16 (17–24)

The ground was dry and cracked. It had not rained for years. No plant could grow. All over the countryside, food was hard to find.

God told the prophet Elijah to go to the town called Zarephath. There he would meet a woman who would feed him. So Elijah left for Zarephath.

When he came to the town gate, he saw a woman gathering sticks for a fire. *This must be the woman*, thought Elijah. "Take this cup, and bring me water to drink," Elijah said to her. As she turned to get the cupful of water, Elijah called, "And bring a piece of bread."

A request for water and bread in a place where it had not rained for so long? What was Elijah thinking?

The woman looked at Elijah and said, "I have no food. I was gathering these few sticks to build a fire. Then I would take the last flour from my jar and make a bit of food for my son and me. After that, we will starve."

"Don't worry," said Elijah. "Do as I say. Then you can make food for you and your son. The God of Israel has said that your flour jar and your oil bottle will never be empty until the rain comes and there will be food again."

The woman did what Elijah said. To her surprise, the flour jar and the oil bottle were never empty. Elijah, the woman, and her son were never hungry.

After some days, the woman's son became sick. The woman was sure he was dying.

"Are you angry with me? Did you come so my son would die?" the woman shouted at Elijah.

"Let me take your son to my room," Elijah said. Elijah took the boy to his room and prayed for him. God heard Elijah's prayer, and the boy got better.

When Elijah and the boy went to the woman, she said, "Now I know that you really are a man of God."

Prayer: God, thank you for prophets like Elijah, who trusted you. We want to trust you too. Amen.

(Sunday between June 12 and June 18 inclusive)

Dinner at Simon's House
Luke 7:36–8:3*

A Pharisee named Simon invited Jesus to his house for dinner. When Jesus arrived and sat at the table, a woman carrying a stone jar of perfumed oil came in. She had not been invited by Simon. She sat at Jesus' feet and washed his feet with her tears. She dried Jesus' feet with her long hair and poured the expensive perfumed oil on his feet.

When Simon saw the woman, whom he had not invited, he said to himself, "Why is Jesus allowing her to do this? He must know I wouldn't have invited her. Surely he knows she is a sinner."

"Simon, I have something to say to you," said Jesus.

"Yes, what is it?" asked Simon.

"Two men owed money to a certain lender," began Jesus. "One man owed a lot of money, but the other man owed just a few coins. Neither man could pay the lender what they owed, so the lender told them they didn't have to pay him. Which of these men will love the lender more?"

---

*A similar story is told when Jesus visits the home of Simon the leper (Matt. 26:6–13). John's version of the story (12:1–11) takes place in the home of Martha, Mary, and Lazarus just before Jesus enters Jerusalem. In that story, Mary washes his feet.

"I think it would be the man who owed the lender the most money," said Simon.

"You are right," said Jesus. "See this woman? When I got here, you didn't offer me water to wash my feet, but she washed them with her tears. You didn't greet me with a kiss, but she has not stopped kissing my feet. You didn't put oil on my head, but she has poured perfumed oil on my feet. I can tell you that all her sins will be forgiven because she has shown great love to me. The one who is forgiven little loves little."

Turning to the woman, Jesus said, "Your sins are forgiven."

The other dinner guests had watched and listened to this exchange and said to one another, "Who is this who forgives sins?"

Still speaking to the woman, Jesus said, "Your faith has saved you. Go in peace."

Surely the woman left smiling.

Prayer: God, we rejoice that you forgive us, no matter what we do. Amen.

(Sunday between June 19 and June 25 inclusive)

On the Mountain
1 Kings 19:1–4 (5–7), 8–15a

A few weeks ago, you heard about how Elijah set up a contest between the Lord God of Israel and Baal. Of course, the Lord God won, and the Israelites returned to worshiping the Lord God, but that wasn't the end of the story.

King Ahab went back to the palace and told Queen Jezebel what happened on Mount Carmel. After that contest, all of the prophets of Baal died. The queen, who was already upset with Elijah, was really angry now because she worshiped Baal. She sent a note to him that said, "By this time tomorrow, I am going to destroy you as the prophets of Baal were destroyed."

When Elijah read that note, he was afraid, so afraid that he and his servant ran away. They went to a place called Beersheba. Elijah told his servant to wait there, and Elijah walked for one whole day into the desert wilderness. When the sun began to set, Elijah sat down under a tree, the only one in the desert.

"Lord God, I have had it. Just let me die here under this tree. I am no better than anyone else." Exhausted, Elijah laid down and fell asleep. Then a messenger from God tapped Elijah on the shoulder. "Get up and eat."

Right next to his head, Elijah found flatbread baking on hot stones and a jar of water. Elijah ate and drank. Then he laid down again, sure that he was going to die. The messenger of God came a second time, tapped Elijah on the shoulder, and said, "Get up and eat." Elijah sat up, saw the bread and water, and ate and drank.

After that, Elijah was able to wander in the desert wilderness for forty days and nights until he reached Mount Horeb, God's holy mountain. He went into a cave when it was night. He heard a voice say, "Why are you here, Elijah?"

"Well, I have been strong for God, but the Israelites have forgotten God. I am the only prophet of the Lord God left. They want to kill me too."

The voice said to Elijah, "Stand outside the cave on the mountain. God is coming by."

Elijah went out and waited. A strong wind blew, so strong that parts of the mountain fell off. But no sign of God. Then there was an earthquake and the mountain shook. But no sign of God. After the earthquake, fire blew by Elijah. Still no sign of God. When the fire was gone, there was nothing. Silence. Elijah wrapped his coat over his face. A voice said, "Why are you here, Elijah?"

The Lord God said, "Go back, Elijah. Anoint a new king and anoint a prophet to follow you." Elijah went back and anointed Hazael as king and Elisha to follow him as God's prophet.

Prayer: God, just as you showed Elijah, show us when and where to look for you. Amen.

(Sunday between June 26 and July 2 inclusive)

Elijah's Coat
2 Kings 2:1–2, 6–14

In the Bible story last week, God told Elijah to anoint someone as the prophet of God who would come after him. Elijah appointed Elisha and set about showing Elisha how to be God's prophet. The two men became good friends.

One day, as Elijah and Elisha were leaving Gigal, Elijah said, "Stay here, Elisha. The Lord God has told me to go to Bethel." Elisha didn't want to stay behind, so he said, "As long as you are alive, I won't leave you." So both Elijah and Elisha went to Bethel.

At Bethel, a group of prophets said to Elisha, "Do you know that the Lord God is going to take Elijah from you today?"

"Yes, but don't talk about it," said Elisha.

Then Elijah said to Elisha, "Stay here; the Lord God has told me to go to Jericho."

Elisha said again, "As long as you are alive, I won't leave you." So together they went to Jericho.

A group of prophets at Jericho took Elisha aside. "The Lord God is going to take Elijah from you today."

"Yes, I know, but don't talk about it," said Elisha.

Elijah came to Elisha and said, "The Lord God has told me to go to the Jordan River, but you stay here."

Once more, Elisha said, "As long as you are alive, I won't leave you." So the two men went to the Jordan River. This time, fifty prophets followed them at a distance.

Elijah and Elisha stood at the Jordan River. Elijah took his coat and rolled it up. When he hit the water with it, the water divided so the men could walk across the river.

On the other side of the river, Elijah said, "What do you want from me before I am taken away?"

"Give me double your spirit," answered Elisha.

"That's a hard one," said Elijah. "If you see me when I'm taken away, you will have it. If you don't see me, you won't."

Then they walked along the riverbank, talking. All of a sudden, a chariot and horses that looked as if they were on fire swooped down between them, and Elijah was taken away in a strong wind!

"Father," cried Elisha. "It's the chariot and horses of Israel!" When he could no longer see Elijah, Elisha tore his clothes in two. Then he picked up Elijah's coat. He hit the water with it and the water divided. Elisha walked across the river. The fifty prophets saw him and shouted, "Elijah's spirit is on Elisha!"

Now Elisha knew what he had to do.

Prayer: God, you have always provided leaders for your people, even today. Thank you. Amen.

A Cure for Naaman
2 Kings 5:1–14

Naaman was a powerful general in Aram's army. Nobody messed with him. But Naaman had red splotches all over his body, and they itched like crazy. Nothing helped.

A Hebrew girl had been captured in one of Naaman's raids and was now the servant of Naaman's wife. She saw how miserable Naaman was. She said to Naaman's wife, "I think that if my master went to see Elisha, a prophet of God in Samaria, he would be healed of this terrible skin disease."

Soon after that, Naaman went to the king of Aram and told him what the servant girl told his wife.

"Go, Naaman," said the king. "I will give you a letter of introduction to the king of Israel."

Naaman packed animals with silver, gold, and many changes of clothing, and off he went to Samaria.

When he got there, he took his letter to the king of Israel. The king read the letter, "This is my servant Naaman. I sent him so you can cure him of his terrible skin disease."

The king got the wrong idea. Afraid this was a sneaky way to attack, he tore his clothes. "What?" said the king, "Am I to cure this man, or does the king of Aram want to fight me?"

When Elisha, the prophet of God, heard that a letter from the king of Aram had made the king of Israel rip his clothes, he sent a message to the king, "Why are you so upset? Send the man to me to be healed."

Naaman went to Elisha's house, along with his many animals carrying the silver, gold, and many changes of clothing. Elisha didn't come out, but sent this message to Naaman, "Go to the Jordan River and wash seven times. Then your skin will be like new."

Naaman was angry. "I have come all this way. This prophet won't even come out to see me, but he tells me to wash in the river seven times. I won't do it! I could have washed in the rivers back home."

The servants who had traveled with Naaman tried to calm him down. "Master, if the prophet had told you to do a difficult task, wouldn't you have done it? Then, why not do this simple task of washing in the river seven times?"

Thinking more clearly now, Naaman went to the Jordan River and washed himself seven times. One, two, three, four, five, six . . . and after the seventh time, Naaman's skin was like new. How amazing!

Prayer: God, sometimes we make following you more difficult than it needs to be. Help us keep it simple. Amen.

❧ PROPER 10 ❧
(Sunday between July 10 and July 16 inclusive)

An Example of Caring
Luke 10:25–37

Jesus was sitting with his disciples when a lawyer, an expert in God's law, came to him. He wanted to test Jesus with a question. "Teacher, what must I do to live with God forever?" he asked.

"What is written in God's law? What do you think it means?" asked Jesus. Surely a lawyer could answer that question.

"You must love God with all your heart, with all your strength, and with all your mind, and love your neighbor as yourself," answered the lawyer.

"Perfect," said Jesus. "Do what you have just said."

But the lawyer wanted to push Jesus a bit more, so he asked, "Who is my neighbor?"

Jesus answered him with this story:

"A man was walking from Jerusalem to Jericho. He was alone, and the road was lonely. Robbers who were hiding behind big rocks attacked him. They beat him and took his clothes and everything he had. The robbers left the man bleeding on the side of the road.

"Not long after that a priest came along the same road.

But when he saw the man bleeding, he walked on the other side of the road to avoid him.

"Before long, a temple worker came by the man, who looked like he was dead. The temple worker crossed to the other side of the road to get around the man too.

"Then a Samaritan man came along the road. Now Jews and Samaritans did not like each other, not at all. They went out of their way to stay apart. So this is where the story gets interesting. When this Samaritan man saw the man bleeding on the side of the road, he stopped. The Samaritan man put bandages on the man's wounds. He carefully lifted the man onto his donkey. He took the man to an inn and told the innkeeper to care for the man. He left money with the innkeeper and said, 'When I come back this way, I will pay anything more you need to spend for this man's care.'"

Jesus looked at the lawyer and asked, "Who in the story was the neighbor?"

"Well, the Samaritan man who stopped and cared for the man who was robbed," said the lawyer.

"You are right. Go and care for others as he did," said Jesus.

Prayer: God, maybe we don't see people bleeding on the side of the road, but we hear about people who need help every day. Give us the courage to help them. Amen.

Two Sisters
Luke 10:38–42

The Bible doesn't have many stories about where Jesus stayed as he and the disciples traveled around the countryside. However, there is one family who seemed to be good friends with Jesus.

The family was two sisters and a brother. They lived in a village called Bethany. Once, when Jesus and the disciples were traveling, they stopped to visit Mary and Martha. There is no mention of the brother Lazarus in this story, so perhaps he wasn't home. Of course, Jesus couldn't call or text ahead to let them know he and the disciples were coming to visit.

When Jesus arrived, Martha welcomed him to her home. Her sister Mary immediately sat down on the floor near Jesus to hear his stories and accounts of his travels.

Meanwhile, Martha was bustling around preparing food for the guests. After all, it isn't every day that thirteen people show up at your door; a proper welcome included offering them food.

Probably a little annoyed at her sister for not helping, Martha stepped in front of Jesus, "Lord, does it make any difference to you that I am getting this whole meal ready by myself and that my sister isn't doing a thing? Tell her to help me."

"Oh, Martha," Jesus answered. "You are hurrying around and worrying about many things. Only one thing is important. Mary has chosen to sit with me. This time won't be taken away from her."

Strangely, the story in the Bible ends there. I wonder what Martha did next. I wonder if Mary helped her with the meal. I wonder what Jesus meant.

Prayer: God, show us the way to learn from your words and to live in your ways. Amen.

❧ PROPER 12 ❧
(Sunday between July 24 and July 30 inclusive)

Teaching about Prayer
Luke 11:1–13

The disciples had seen Jesus go off by himself to pray many times. But apparently Jesus never talked with them about how to pray as he did. Finally, one of the disciples said, "Master, teach us how to pray. John the baptizer taught his followers how to pray."

It seems that the request was all that was needed, for Jesus immediately answered, "When you pray to God, say:

> Father, your name is holy,
> > Your kingdom come.
> > Give us food every day.
> > And forgive our sins,
> > > for we ourselves forgive everyone.
> > And do not bring us to the time of trial."*

After teaching this prayer, Jesus told the disciples more about prayer, saying, "Suppose you go to a friend's house in the middle of the night and say, 'Friend, give me three loaves of bread. A friend who is traveling has just arrived, and I

---

*An alternative is to say the words your congregation uses for the Lord's Prayer.

want to feed him.' Suppose your friend says, 'It's too late. I am in bed. Don't bother me!' I would say that even if your friend didn't *want* to get up and help you, because he is your friend, he will get up and help you because you came so late at night. So I tell you: Ask and you will receive. Seek and you will find. Knock and the door will be opened. What parent would give a snake to a child who asks for a fish? Or would you give your child a dangerous scorpion? No, you give good gifts to your children. The same is true of God who gives you the Holy Spirit."

Now the disciples had a lot to think about praying to God. Ask, seek, knock. You will receive, find, and the door will be opened.

Prayer: God, we will pray to you, knowing that you will answer our prayers with good gifts to us. Amen.

(Sunday between July 31 and August 6 inclusive)

A Man's Request
Luke 12:13–21

Often when Jesus was teaching large crowds of people, someone had a question for him. On this day, a man called out, "Teacher, tell my brother to share the money from our father with me!"

Jesus walked over to the man, "Whoa! Who appointed me the judge between you and your brother?"

Then, paying no attention to the question from the man, Jesus told this story:

"A rich farmer had a large crop one year. So much grain was coming in from his fields that he didn't know where to store it. The farmer said to himself, 'What will I do with all this grain?' After thinking about this nice problem for a while, he decided to tear down his barns and build bigger barns.

"'I will store all my grain in them. When I have stored up enough for several years, I will take a long vacation. I will eat good food and enjoy myself.'

"But God said to this rich farmer, 'You fool! Tonight you will die. Now who will get all the things you have stored for yourself when you are dead and gone?'"

After the story, Jesus said, "This is what happens when people store up their riches but pay no attention to God."

Did Jesus answer the man's question about the money from their father, or not?

Prayer: God, help us discover how to pay attention to you. Amen.

Hard Times
Hebrews 11:1–3, 8–16

A leader of the followers of Jesus sat in prayer one day. He had heard of the terrible trouble followers of Jesus were having in another city. Like this leader, they were Jews—or Hebrews—people who had known the Lord God all their lives. They believed that God sent Jesus to them, which got them into trouble with people who did not believe this. They were beaten and called awful names. People who were against them told the Roman officials that the followers of Jesus were creating disturbances. Life was terrible for these followers of Jesus.

This leader prayed, asking God what could be done for Jesus' followers in that city. *Aha*, he thought, *I'll send a letter to encourage them and to remind them of all the people who had trusted in God, no matter what.*

Unlike other letters in the Bible, this letter doesn't begin with who wrote it or to whom it was written. So we don't know where these Hebrew followers of Jesus lived. Instead, this is how the letter to the Hebrews begins: "Before Jesus was born, God spoke through prophets, people who gave God's message to the people in many ways. Then God sent Jesus to tell about God and show how to live in God's ways. Jesus,

God's Son, has all the brightness of God's glory and is like God in every way."

This unknown church leader, writing to Jewish followers of Jesus in an unknown city, wrote a very long letter, one of the longest in the Bible. This leader wanted the people to remember their ancestors, such as Abraham and Sarah, who had such faith in God that they traveled to a new land. They trusted God even when they couldn't imagine what God told them would happen. But when Sarah had a baby boy, Isaac, they knew that God kept those promises.

Today, when we read the letter to the Hebrews, we remember that we can trust God, because God keeps promises.

Prayer: God, we want to remember each day that you love us and that you keep your promises. Amen.

(Sunday between August 14 and August 20 inclusive)

A Great Cloud of Witnesses
Hebrews 11:29–12:2

You heard last week about the unknown church leader who wrote the letter to the Hebrews, urging them to remember all the people who have trusted God and had faith in God.

In this letter, the church leader recalled:

> "By faith, Moses and the Israelites crossed through
> the Red Sea on dry land to escape slavery in
> Egypt, but the Egyptian army was destroyed.
> "By faith, Joshua and the Israelites marched
> around the walls of Jericho until they fell down.
> "By faith, Daniel was not harmed when he was
> thrown into the lions' den.
> "By faith, others were hurt and made fun of, but
> their faith kept them strong."

Then the writer encouraged the readers to remember this great crowd of people, who are like a cloud of witnesses surrounding them, helping them keep their faith strong.

Those same words are for the church—us—today. This great cloud of witnesses is even bigger for us because so many people have been added to it since the letter was sent to the Hebrews.*

Prayer: God, we are strengthened by the faithful people who stood strong with you through good and bad. Amen.

*Names of people from your congregation or church history can be added here.

(Sunday between August 21 and August 27 inclusive)

Healed on the Sabbath
Luke 13:10–17

It's back to the Gospel of Luke for the story today. As before, Jesus and the twelve disciples were traveling all around Galilee. Sometimes others were with them. Luke names Mary Magdalene, Joanna, and Susanna. The news about Jesus spread from one person to the next, from one village to the next. No posters or ads, just one person telling another about this man who taught and healed with a special authority.

Jesus often taught in synagogues, where the Jews in the village gathered to study God's Word, what we call the Old Testament. Jesus would read a passage from a scroll and then explain it. On this day, he was teaching in a synagogue. Among the congregation was one woman who had been crippled for eighteen years. She was so bent over that she couldn't see the trees or even the faces of the people around her. She could see only the ground because she could not stand up straight.

Jesus saw this woman and asked her to come to him. He said, "Woman, you are no longer sick." Then he placed his hands on her, and she stood up straight and tall. At once, she gave thanks and praised God.

This was all fine, except that this happened on the Sabbath day, when no work was to be done. The synagogue leader watched all this and became very angry. Healing on the Sabbath? Never!

The synagogue leader hurried over to Jesus and the woman and said, "Six days you have to heal and work. Why must you disobey God's laws and heal on the Sabbath day?"

Jesus, just as angry as the synagogue leader, said, "Nonsense! Don't you untie your donkey and lead it to get a drink on the Sabbath day? Then shouldn't I heal a Jewish woman who has been crippled for eighteen years on the Sabbath day?"

The synagogue leader and the people who agreed with him looked down at the ground, ashamed of themselves. But the people in the synagogue who had seen the woman healed gave shouts of joy.

Prayer: God, your love through Jesus is wonderful to see. Amen.

(Sunday between August 28 and September 3 inclusive)

Good Hosts and Guests
Luke 14:1, 7–14

One Sabbath day, Jesus was invited to dinner at the home of a leader of the Pharisees, the experts in God's law. The Pharisees were carefully watching Jesus to see if he made mistakes in God's teachings.

Jesus watched the people as they scrambled to get the best seats at the table. Then he told the dinner guests this story: "When someone invites you to a wedding dinner, don't go straight to a seat near the bride and groom in the place of honor. That place may be saved for someone else. If you sit there, the host will come to you and ask you to move. How embarrassing! Instead, sit in the least important seat. Then your host may come to you and say, 'Friend, come sit in a better seat.' By his words, you will be honored in front of everyone. People who make themselves important will be last, and people who do not make themselves important will be first."

Jesus also had some advice for the host of the dinner. "When you give a lunch or a dinner, don't invite people like you, your family, or rich neighbors. No, invite people who are poor, who cannot walk, or who are blind. You will be blessed because they cannot invite you in return."

The guests and the host of that dinner had much to think about. I wonder what the next dinner party was like.

Prayer: God, we want to be hosts and guests who follow Jesus' ways. Amen.

(Sunday between September 4 and September 10 inclusive)

To Follow Jesus
Luke 14:25–33

The number of people traveling with Jesus was growing. Now a large crowd walked with him. Some people walked to the next village; others walked a longer way. Jesus looked at the people. He wondered, *Do they really understand what it means to follow me?* Jesus wasn't sure, so he said to the crowd, "You must give up everything to follow me. You must live as I live."

Just in case, they didn't get it, Jesus continued, "If you were building a tower so you could watch over your fields or grape vines, and you found you couldn't finish it because you ran out of money, wouldn't your neighbors make fun of you? When you went to the marketplace, they would point at you and whisper, 'That one started building a tower in his field and couldn't finish it.' If you were a king and wanted to go to war against another king, wouldn't you send spies to see how many soldiers the other king had? Who would be so foolish to attack a king who had lots more soldiers than he did? Instead, the smart king would go and try to make a peace treaty with the other king. This is like following me. You have to give up all the things you have to be my disciple."

People looked at one another. Was the man building the tower to use all his money to finish it? Was the king to make a peace treaty, even if he had to give up his kingdom? What does Jesus expect us to give up?

I wonder if some people went home then.

Prayer: God, as we try to follow Jesus and be his disciples, give us courage. Amen.

(Sunday between September 11 and September 17 inclusive)

A Sheep and a Coin
Luke 15:1–10

On this day, Jesus stopped to teach the crowd around him. Some tax collectors and other people that the Jewish leaders thought did bad things were in the crowd. The Pharisees who followed God's laws perfectly and other experts in God's law were also there. They were disgusted that Jesus would be around such folks as tax collectors. They grumbled, "This man welcomes people who don't follow God's laws. He even eats meals with them."

Looking right at the group of Pharisees and law experts, Jesus told them this story: "If you have one hundred sheep and one evening you count them . . . 98, 99. You can't believe it, so you count again . . . 95, 96, 97, 98, 99. One sheep is missing! Wouldn't you leave the ninety-nine sheep in the field and go looking for the lost sheep? You would look in bushes and behind rocks. You would look in ditches and on the hills. When you finally found the lost sheep, you would bring it back to the ninety-nine sheep. Then you would go to your neighbors and say, 'I have found my lost sheep. Let's have a party!'

"That is just how happy God is when someone who has strayed away from God's ways returns.

"Or think about this. A woman has ten coins. She keeps them in the same place. But one day, she counts her coins . . . 1, 2, 3, 4, 5, 6, 7, 8, 9. *That can't be right*, she thinks. So she counts the coins again . . . 1, 2, 3, 4, 5, 6, 7, 8, 9. Now she is really worried. She sweeps the floor, reaching into all the corners and under the furniture. She lights a lamp so she can look inside the cupboards. Finally, she finds the missing coin. She, too, goes to her neighbors and says, 'I've found my lost coin. Come, celebrate with me.'

"That is the kind of joy that all God's angels feel when one person returns to God's ways."

Prayer: God, even when we forget to follow your ways or to trust you, we know that you welcome us back. Amen.

(Sunday between September 18 and September 24 inclusive)

A Letter to Timothy
1 Timothy 2:1–7

Paul met the young man Timothy in Lystra. Timothy's mother was a believer in Jesus Christ, but his father was Greek and not a believer. The people in the church in Lystra said good things about Timothy and his strong faith in Jesus Christ. At that time Paul was traveling alone, so he invited Timothy to go with him.

When Paul and Timothy went to the region of Macedonia, he left Timothy in the town of Ephesus, where they had begun a church. Timothy could help these new believers. While Timothy was there, Paul wrote to him, giving him instructions on how to teach the new believers there.

In the First Letter to Timothy in our Bible, Paul writes about prayer. Listen to what Paul says:

"First, above everything else, I ask you to pray for everyone. Give prayers of thanks, prayers that ask for help, and prayers of praise to God. Pray for government leaders and everyone who has power over you. Pray that they will lead peace-filled lives. Then we can live peace-filled lives too. When we pray like this, God is happy. God also wants everyone to know the truth and be saved."

That is what Timothy did, and that is what Timothy taught the people in the church in Ephesus. Now Paul is telling you this too: pray for everyone.

Prayer: God, we pray for everyone—our families and friends, our church, people who are sick or lonely, people who are hungry or homeless. We pray for the leaders of all nations. And we pray for ourselves. Amen.

Good Words for Timothy
1 Timothy 6:6–19

Remember last week we heard about Timothy, whom Paul met in Lystra. Timothy became one of Paul's best leaders, and Paul trusted Timothy enough to leave him with new churches to continue to teach the people. You may also remember that one city where Timothy stayed behind to teach the people was Ephesus. There is so much to teach new believers in Jesus Christ, people who never saw or heard Jesus teach. Timothy had lots to do. So Timothy was relieved to get a letter from Paul. Paul was his teacher, and his letters were almost like having Paul next to him talking about Jesus and living as Jesus taught.

Last week, the part of the letter we heard was about prayer; pray for everyone. Near the end of the letter, Paul reminds Timothy of how to live so he stays close to God. Listen to Paul's words, "Being close to God can make you rich, but not rich in money or lots of things. Being close to God makes you happy with what you already have. When you were born, you didn't have one thing. When you die, you can't take anything with you. So be happy with the food and clothing you have. When you try to get too many things, you are tempted to do things that hurt other people. If you love money, you will be headed for lots of trouble.

"You, Timothy, should go far away from that kind of trouble. Instead, seek to be right with God, faithful to God, and work at being loving, dependable, and gentle."

Once again, Paul's words to Timothy are good words for us. This week, let's work at being loving, dependable, and gentle.

Prayer: God, help us be loving, dependable, and gentle this week. Amen.

(Sunday between October 2 and October 8 inclusive)

Like a Dear Son
2 Timothy 1:1–14

Paul wrote at least one more letter to Timothy while Timothy was in Ephesus. In our Bible it is called Second Timothy. It begins like this: "From Paul, an apostle of Christ Jesus, called by God to tell about the promise of life that is in Christ Jesus.

"To Timothy, who is like a dear son to me."

Paul is in prison now, so there is no chance that he can come to visit the church in Ephesus, where he has many friends and, of course, Timothy. Paul remembers the strong faith in Christ Jesus that Timothy's mother, Eunice, and his grandmother Lois had. He is happy that this same strong faith is in Timothy. Paul writes to encourage Timothy to stand firm in this faith: "God gave us a spirit that is powerful and loving, not one that is shy and weak. So don't be ashamed to tell others about Christ Jesus or about me in prison. God's power will help you tell everyone this good news of Christ Jesus.

"I was called by God to be an apostle, a messenger, a teacher of this good news. You have been called, too, to teach what you learned from me. Hold on to what you know and the love that is in Christ Jesus."

Paul's words of encouragement for Timothy are words of encouragement for us—children, women, and men—today. We can also hold onto the love that is in Christ Jesus.

Prayer: God, send us your Spirit to keep our faith strong. Amen.

(Sunday between October 9 and October 15 inclusive)

One Thank You
Luke 17:11–19

This story takes place before Jesus came to Jerusalem. Jesus and the disciples were traveling from village to village, from town to town, stopping only for Jesus to teach about God and to heal people. They were along the border between Galilee and Samaria. It's important to know, for this story, that the Samaritans, the people who lived in Samaria, and the Jews, who lived in Galilee, did not like each other, not one bit. In fact, they wouldn't talk to each other, and many Jews wouldn't even go into Samaria. So Jesus was on the border between these two countries, but he was on the Galilee side, the Jewish side.

As Jesus and the disciples came close to a village near the border, ten men with a skin disease came toward Jesus. In those days, people would walk the other direction so they wouldn't come close to someone with a skin disease. They called such people unclean and made them live outside the village or town. Having lived with the skin disease for a long time, the people stopped before they got close to Jesus. "Jesus," they shouted, "have mercy on us!"

When Jesus saw and heard them, he said, "Go to the priests and show them."

What did Jesus mean? The priests wouldn't want to get near them. Then the people looked at their arms and their legs. The skin disease was gone! Yes, they would go to the priests and show them that they were no longer unclean. They could live in the village. They could worship God with everyone else.

One of the people, a man from Samaria, saw that he was cured. He ran to Jesus and fell at his feet. All the while, he shouted praises and thanks to God.

"Weren't ten people healed?" asked Jesus. "Where are the other nine? This Samaritan man was the only one who praised God?"

Jesus looked at the man kneeling at his feet. "Get up and go," said Jesus. "Your faith has made you well."

Prayer: God, when good things happen to us, we will give thanks to you. Amen.

(Sunday between October 16 and October 22 inclusive)

Keep Praying
Luke 18:1–8

Prayer, talking with God, was important to Jesus. In the Gospel of Luke, it is often reported that Jesus went off by himself to pray. Just as Jesus taught the crowds with stories, he also taught his disciples with stories. To encourage them to pray every day, he told them this story: "Once upon a time a judge lived in a city. The whole city knew that this judge didn't care a thing about people, and this judge had no use for God. In that city, there also lived a widow, who had no husband or sons to protect her.

"Someone had treated the widow unfairly, and she wanted things set right. To do that, she went to the judge. She said to the judge, 'Set things right! Give me justice!' The judge refused to do anything.

"But the widow came back, day after day, and each time she said, 'Set things right! Give me justice!'

"Day after day, the judge paid no attention to her and did nothing.

"This continued for many days. 'Set things right! Give me justice!' Nothing from the judge.

"Finally, the judge was sick and tired of seeing and hearing this widow every day. He said, 'I don't care a thing about people, and I have no use for God, but I am tired of this widow. I will set things right and give her justice so she won't bother me anymore!'"

The disciples were quiet and Jesus said to them, "See how this bad judge finally did what was right? Don't you think that God who is good will do even more for you if you ask?"

Prayer: God, we know we are to pray to you every day, just as Jesus taught. Amen.

Two Prayers
Luke 18:9–14

Sometimes Jesus told a story to teach particular people. Jesus told this story to people who thought they were better than other people. See if you can guess who those people were.

"Two people went to the temple to pray. One was a Pharisee. The Pharisee made a big deal of going to the temple. He strutted past others in the street and held his head high. When he went into the temple, he stood in the middle where everyone there could see him praying.

"The other person was a tax collector. Back in those times, tax collectors had no friends. People didn't like them because they collected taxes for the Roman rulers, whom nobody liked or trusted. This tax collector walked to the temple quietly so no one would notice him. He walked softly into the temple and quickly went to a dark corner where he wouldn't be seen.

"The Pharisee prayed with his hands raised high above his head. He spoke loudly, 'God, thank you that I am not like other people, especially that tax collector. I go without food twice a week. I give generously to the temple just as your law says.'

"Over in the corner, the tax collector stood with his head down to his chest. He wouldn't look up to heaven. Instead, he beat his chest with his fists and prayed, 'God, I am a sinner. Show mercy to me.'

"It is true that the tax collector will go home feeling forgiven, but the Pharisee will not. People who lift themselves above others will be brought down. People who know what they have done wrong will be lifted high."

I wonder what the people who thought they were better than other people thought of Jesus' story.

Prayer: God, help us remember that everyone is equal before you. Amen.

Up a Tree
Luke 19:1–10

Jesus and the disciples were headed for Jerusalem. On the way, they went through a town called Jericho. Like every city ruled by the Romans, Jericho had a tax collector. His name was Zacchaeus.

Word spread through the town that Jesus was nearby and headed their way. People who had heard about Jesus' teaching and healing came to the street to watch for him. Zacchaeus was curious about Jesus too. But when he got to the street, he couldn't see over all the people because he was short.

He looked down the street and saw a sycamore tree. He hurried to it and climbed it so he could see Jesus when he walked by.

Now something surprising happened. When Jesus got to the sycamore tree, he stopped. He looked up in the tree at Zacchaeus. Zacchaeus froze. Jesus said, "Zacchaeus, come down from that tree right now. I am going to stay at your house tonight."

Zacchaeus scrambled down from that tree in a hurry. The people who heard what Jesus said muttered, "What! Jesus is going to stay with the tax collector?" (You remember how people hated tax collectors.)

Zacchaeus stood in front of Jesus. "Look, Lord," he said, "I give half of my possessions to the poor. And if I have cheated anyone, I repay four times as much" (v. 8 CEB).

"Zacchaeus," said Jesus. "Mercy has come to your house today, and you are a son of Abraham."

They walked away together to go to Zacchaeus's house. I wonder what the people who muttered thought then.

Prayer: God, we want to welcome Jesus to our houses too. Amen.

⁊ PROPER 27 ⁊

(Sunday between November 6 and November 12 inclusive)

Every Good Word and Act
2 Thessalonians 2:1–5, 13–17

The apostles, including Paul, traveled away from Jerusalem to tell people about the good news of Jesus Christ and God's love. In many places, the people who believed that Jesus was sent by God and was God's Son continued to meet together after the apostle went to another city. But there was no one to teach them or answer their questions about Jesus and God. The believers in these new churches in faraway cities were often lonely, and other people made fun of them or even treated them meanly. So a letter from the apostle who had taught them was a reason to be happy.

The new church in Thessalonica was like that. Some people were treating them badly. Perhaps they wouldn't sell food to them, or, even worse, they told lies about them to the Roman rulers to get them into trouble. The church people still gathered to pray and worship God. They tried to remember what they had been taught about Jesus, but not everyone remembered the same things. Sometimes they argued about what to believe.

When a letter arrived from a church leader, the Thessalonians (that's what the people who lived in Thessalonica were called) eagerly read the letter together.

116

This is from the Second Letter to the Thessalonians in our Bible: "Brothers and sisters, your strong faith continues to grow in spite of the bad ways you are treated because you believe in Christ Jesus. God called all of you through the message of Jesus, in which you must stand firm. May God encourage you and give you strength in every good word or act."

These words are for us too. May God encourage us and strengthen us so we speak good words to people and act in loving ways to everyone.

Prayer: God, we are grateful for the letters, written so long ago. We want your encouragement and strength too. Amen.

Doing What Is Right
2 Thessalonians 3:6–13

L ast week, we heard some words to the church in Thessa-lonica to give them courage to continue to be strong in their belief about Jesus Christ. So one problem the Thessalonian believers were having was with other people, people who did not believe in Jesus, who were mean to them and told lies about them that got them into trouble.

But that wasn't the only problem in the church in Thessalonica. Some people weren't doing their fair share of the work. For example, some people didn't work at all and still expected they would have food to eat. I'm not talking about people who were old or sick; these were people who were healthy and strong. As you can imagine, the people who did work were pretty upset with those who did not. So another part of the Second Letter to the Thessalonians in our Bible is about this problem inside the church: "Brothers and sisters, in the name of Jesus Christ, have nothing to do with people who do not follow the teachings of Jesus. Stay away from lazy people and people who refuse to work. When we were with you, we worked day and night. We didn't have to work because we were your guests, but we wanted to set a good example for you.

"Don't hang out with busybodies, who spend too much time checking up on everyone else and not enough time on following Jesus. For the sake of Jesus Christ, won't those people stop what they are doing and work so there is food on the table for everyone? But, no matter what, don't get tired of doing what is right."

Now there's good advice for everyone even today: don't get tired of doing what is right.

Prayer: God, give us strength and strong faith so that we do not get tired of doing what is right. Amen.

Good and Bad Shepherds
Jeremiah 23:1–6

Jeremiah was a prophet of God. In those days, God spoke to the prophets and gave them messages for the people of God, the Israelites. The Old Testament part of our Bible has many books of the words that were given to prophets.

Jeremiah was the son of a priest. The first time God spoke to Jeremiah and told him he was to be a "prophet to all nations," Jeremiah answered, "Not me, God, I am just a child."

But God answered, "Don't be afraid. I am with you. I will put the words in your mouth."

The words God gave Jeremiah weren't always happy words. Often the words made the people of God angry. But the words also gave hope to the Israelites, if they would just listen. Once, God gave Jeremiah words about good and bad shepherds. But the words were really about the kings of Israel. Listen carefully and think about what the kings might think about these words: "You shepherds who send the sheep off in all directions, watch out! These are God's words. This is how you 'tend' my people. You drive them away north, south, east, and west. You don't take good care of them, so I will make you sorry. I will gather the sheep myself. I will bring them to

120

my good pasture. Then they will be healthy and have many lambs. I will find shepherds who will care for them with love. Then my sheep will not be afraid and nothing bad will happen to them. And none of them will be missing."

See why Jeremiah had a hard time with the kings?

Prayer: God, show us the way to find good leaders who will care for us with love. Amen.

STORIES FOR SPECIAL SUNDAYS

Selection of Matthais
Acts 1:15–26

The last time the disciples saw Jesus was on the Mount of Olives, about a day's walk from Jerusalem. When Jesus left them to be with God, the disciples headed back to Jerusalem. When they got there, they agreed to meet in an upstairs room where they were staying. In the room were the apostles: Peter, James, John, Andrew, Philip, Thomas, Bartholomew, Matthew, James the son of Alphaeus, Simon, and Judas the son of James. Some women were also in the room, including the mother of Jesus, along with a crowd of other disciples.

Not in the room was Judas Iscariot. Judas had left them after Jesus was arrested. They had not seen him since that time.

Peter stood up. "Brothers and sisters," he said, "we must select someone to take the place of Judas. This should be someone who has been with us since the beginning, from the time Jesus was baptized, and who has seen him as the resurrected Lord."

Everyone looked around. Who might this be? Two men in the room had been with them from the beginning. They were Joseph, also called Barsabbas or Justus, and Matthias.

The people in that room believed that God would show

them the way, so they prayed, "God, you know everything. You know our deepest thoughts. Show us clearly which one of these men is the right choice."

The people cast lots, which means that they threw two stones with markings on them, which were used for making decisions. Matthias was chosen and became the twelfth apostle. Now their number was complete, and they would be ready to teach, to heal, and to baptize when they received the gift of the Holy Spirit.

We don't cast lots to choose leaders today, but the Nominating Committee did pray as they considered leaders for our church. The people they chose and who this congregation elected will be recognized today.

Prayer: God, thank you for the good leaders you have provided for your people, including leaders for this church. Amen.

The Widow's Coins
Luke 21:1–4

Remember when Jesus rode into Jerusalem on a donkey? We call that day Palm Sunday. That night Jesus and the disciples left Jerusalem, but each day he came back to teach at the temple. Many people listened to him, and the Jewish leaders listened very carefully.

On one of those days, the Jewish leaders, who knew all the religious laws and taught that every law had to obeyed, were watching Jesus. From time to time, they would ask Jesus a question to see if they could stump him or cause him to say something wrong.

On that day, Jesus and the disciples were standing in the temple near the place where people came to put in their money offerings for the temple and to God.

Jesus wasn't teaching, but he was looking around at the people and watching what they were doing. He saw some rich people come with their bags of coins for the temple offering. They dropped the bags of coins into the box. Clank, ka-ching, clang—the bags of coins made so much noise that people turned to see who was putting the money in the offering box.

Jesus continued to watch the people bring their offerings. He saw a poor widow, a woman with no husband to care for her, which was important in those days. This poor widow quietly dropped one, two coins into the temple offering box. You couldn't even hear them fall to the bottom.

Pointing to the woman, Jesus said to his disciples, "See that poor widow. The two copper coins that she has given are far more than the rich people with their bags of coins. The rich people gave from the extra money they had. The poor widow gave all that she had for food and to live on."

Two copper coins more than a bag of money? What strange math Jesus used.

Prayer: God, help me understand the value of my gifts, however small. Amen.

Solomon Builds the Temple
1 Kings 8:18–66

King David wanted to build a house for God, a place to keep the Ark, or Box, of the Covenant. But God said, "No, thanks, King David, I don't need a house. But when your son Solomon is king, he may build a house for me."

King David was disappointed, but at least his son would build the temple, the house for God.

When Solomon became king, he built the temple, and a magnificent building it was, made with huge stones and beautiful, carved cedar wood walls. Inside the temple was covered with gold, completely! It was the most magnificent building the people had ever seen.

When everything was finished, King Solomon brought together all the leaders of Israel to bring the Ark of the Covenant to the temple. And when it was in the temple, the cloud of God, God's Spirit, filled the temple.

King Solomon stood before the people. Then he fell on his knees and prayed to God. "Lord God of Israel, you are the God above all gods. You keep your promises to us. You promised my father, David, that I would build this temple for you. Still we know that you are bigger than creation and will not fit in this temple. Listen to my prayer that you will always watch over this temple. Promise to be with us always."

King Solomon prayed and prayed. When he stood up, he blessed the people: "May the Lord our God be with us, as God was with all the people before us. May you be faithful to God with all your heart and follow God's commandments."

The people celebrated for fourteen days. After the fourteenth day, they returned to their tents, happy and glad for all that had happened.

When our church was built, the people also celebrated, although probably not for fourteen days. They thanked God and promised to be faithful to God too.

Prayer: God, you kept your promise to Solomon and the Israelites, and you kept your promise to us. Thank you. Amen.

Jesus Sends the Disciples Two by Two
Matthew 9:35–10:8

Jesus traveled from city to city and village to village. Wherever he went, he taught in the synagogue, the Jewish house of learning and worship. Wherever he went, people who were sick came to him to be healed. So many people wanted to hear him and see him, too many people for him to see and teach and heal.

Jesus called twelve men to be his special disciples. These men had traveled with Jesus from city to city and from village to village. They would help him teach and heal. Jesus gave them the power to do what he did.

Then he said to them, "Go to the lost ones of Israel, not to the others. Tell them that the kingdom of heaven is near. As you give this message, heal sick people, whether they have a skin disease or some other illness. Don't let anyone pay you because you have been given this power to heal without paying for it. Take only what you need with you. If people speak badly to you, leave their town and go to another one. But if people are good to you, stay with them and bless them with peace."

Today we are sending some of our people to help the

people in another town.* We will send them with our prayers and blessings, just as Jesus sent those first disciples.

Prayer: God, you called people from the beginning to take your word to new places. Be with those we send in your name today. Amen.

---

*You may personalize this sentence to describe your situation.

CPSIA information can be obtained at www.ICGtesting.com
Printed in the USA
BVOW08s1600110716

455131BV00001BA/28/P